The Book of Nehemiah

Sermon Commentary Series

Dr. Brandon J. Crawford

Arete Publishing, LLC

The Book of Nehemiah
Sermon Commentary Series

Copyright © 2025 by Dr. Brandon J. Crawford

Published by Arete Publishing, LLC
www.AretePublishing.com

All rights reserved.

ISBN 978-1-964118-08-6

Scripture quotations taken from the (LSB®) Legacy Standard Bible®, Copyright © 2021 by The Lockman Foundation. Used by permission. All rights reserved. Managed in partnership with Three Sixteen Publishing Inc., LSBible.org, and 316publishing.com.

No portion of this book may be reproduced in any form, or by any means electronic or mechanical, including photocopying, recording, or by any information storage or retrieval system, without written permission from the publisher and author, except in the case of brief quotations in articles and reviews, or as provided by U.S. copyright law.

Contents

Preface	IV
1. Rise Up and Rebuild	1
2. Rebuilding Our Prayer Lives	10
3. Rebuilding Our Moral Courage	20
4. Rebuilding Our Missional Focus	31
5. Rebuilding Our Synergy	41
6. Rebuilding in the Face of Opposition	51
7. Rebuilding Our Institutional Integrity	62
8. Rebuilding with Unbreakable Leadership	72
9. Rebuilding Corporate Worship	83
10. Rebuilding Godly Households	94
11. Rebuilding Our Resolve Part One	104
12. Rebuilding Our Resolve Part Two	114
13. Rebuilding with Godly Leadership	124
14. Rebuilding Our Vigilance	133
About the Author	144

Preface

The Book of Nehemiah stands as a powerful testament to the grace of God, the resilience of His people, and the transformative work of God-wrought faith in the face of adversity. As we journey through the pages of this ancient text, we find not just the story of rebuilding Jerusalem's walls but also the spiritual reawakening of a people called to restoration. This commentary, based on a sermon series entitled *Rise Up and Rebuild,* seeks to uncover the timeless relevance of Nehemiah's leadership, the challenges of rebuilding what was broken, and the call to stand firm in the face of opposition.

In the unfolding narrative, Nehemiah's example of courage, prayer, and perseverance amidst difficulty offers valuable lessons for church leaders. His unwavering commitment to God's purposes, his humility in seeking God's guidance, and his practical steps in mobilizing the people can all serve us well. Yet, Nehemiah's story is not just for leaders. It is also about the restoration of whole communities, the reconciling of a people to God, and the rededication of lives to the divine mission.

This commentary aims to reflect on the themes of faith, leadership, repentance, and communal transformation that emerge from Nehemiah's journey. It draws from the truths shared during the sermon series and seeks to apply these lessons to the lives of believers, encouraging each of us to answer the call to rise up and rebuild.

Chapter One

Rise Up and Rebuild

Reformation begins when a man of God, understanding the needs of the hour, resolves to act no matter the personal cost.

I. Introduction to sermon on Nehemiah 1:1-4. We live in serious times, which call for a serious Church. Unfortunately, few serious churches exist in America today. We have silly churches with ministers who step onto the platform dressed as cartoon characters. Churches that hold "Bring Your Pet to Church Sunday" for a blessing of the animals. Churches that have removed their pulpits from the stage so the audience can better view the band. Churches that know everything about hosting carnivals but nothing about the historic confessions and creeds. Churches that are eager to teach you about the Enneagram but are unwilling to expose you to an extended exposition of God's Word.

In short, the American Church needs a Martin Luther-John Calvin-style Reformation. It needs a revival on the scale that the American colonies experienced in the lead-up to the Revolutionary War. It needs to be rebuilt the way Europe was rebuilt after World War II. This task sounds daunting, and indeed it is, but we can take comfort that God has done this kind of work before. There were other times in history when God's people were at a spiritual low, a beleaguered minority surrounded by a hostile culture, and when it seemed as if there was no hope. But then God started a new work among them, restored their vitality, and brought his Word back to the center of their lives. It happened in the days of Nehemiah.

II. Historical context. If you are unfamiliar with the Book of Nehemiah, it was written about 2,500 years ago on the other side of the world when God's people were still primarily confined to a single nation: Israel. They were at an absolute low point. The problem began generations earlier with their indifference to the Word of God. They did not take it seriously anymore, which started their spiritual drift. And for generations, it continued to worsen. So God raised up prophets to call them back to faithfulness—faithfulness to him and their national covenant. But the people ignored all of these pleas. Finally, it got to the point where the Jewish nation was worshiping false gods, even sacrificing their children to these gods. God finally had no more of it.

He raised up a pagan empire called the Assyrian Empire. In 722 B.C., the Assyrians rolled their war machine through the northern kingdom of Israel, destroying the land and taking all of its people into captivity. Ten of Israel's twelve tribes were lost in that invasion. The two remaining tribes should have learned a lesson from this great tragedy but did not. They continued their downward spiral until finally, in 586 B.C., God raised up a new pagan empire called the Babylonian Empire. This empire marched into the southern kingdom of Judah, where the two tribes of Judah and Benjamin were located, obliterating Jerusalem, the nation's capital. The Babylonians laid waste to the Jewish Temple, destroyed the walls of the city, and then carted off all the people, the best and the brightest of them, back into Babylon.

When the invasion happened, the people of God lost every institution they had always counted on: their Temple, monarchy, land, and holy city—all of it. For 70 long years, they were a scattered remnant in a hostile society. Depressed and despondent, they wondered how they would continue. However, God began a new work among them: He raised up another empire on the world stage, the Persian Empire, with a new king named Cyrus. God used this pagan empire to begin sending his ancient people back to their homeland again. It was remarkable. You see, God is the king of all people, both those who acknowledge him as Lord and those who do not, so if he wants to use a pagan empire and a pagan king to do good for his people, he can do that. And he did so in those days.

The first wave of Jews returned home under the leadership of Zerubbabel and Joshua. Immediately, they got to work rebuilding their temple and planted the seeds of reformation. About 60 years later, another wave of returnees arrived in the Holy Land, led by Ezra, who began to teach the people about God. Ezra expounded the Scriptures to the people and helped to facilitate the renewal of their national covenant with God. The seeds of reformation were taking hold, and a new spiritual life was beginning to emerge, but much work was needed. The reformation needed to be completed, so God raised up Nehemiah. He would send him back to Israel in a third wave of returnees and use him to complete the reformation of his people.

Today, we are beginning our walk through the Book of Nehemiah, which is named after this man. It tells how God used him to lead his people to complete the reformation and a national revival. Though Nehemiah lived and ministered at a time very different from ours and in a different part of the world, our situations are close enough that we can apply the lessons of this book to our time. In Nehemiah's day, God's people were at a spiritual low. In our day, the Church in America is at a spiritual low. However, in Nehemiah's day, God turned things around by sparking a reformation. God can do the same for us today. The Book of Nehemiah will show us how God did it before and how he might do it again. Today, we shall look at Nehemiah 1:1-4, which sets the stage for the rest of our series. It also gives us some principles that characterize the beginning of a reformation.

III. Reformation begins with a man of God. Reformation is always a work of God, who is moving on the hearts of his people, drawing them back to himself and his Word. But God also works through leaders whom he raises up. Reformation can begin when a man or woman of God takes it upon himself or herself to seek God's face and to draw his people back to himself. It really is that simple. God only needs one person to spark a reformation—just one man or woman of God—someone who has been changed by God's grace and who delights in his glory, has a heart for his people, has been captured by his Word, has reforming zeal, and is willing to do the work necessary to lead his people back to life and health. Nehemiah was just such a man.

The Scriptures provide little background information about him. All we have is Nehemiah 1:1, which tells us he was the son of a man called Hacaliah, a name that means "one who waits for the Lord." This passage suggests that Hacaliah's parents were very godly. In those days, people did not choose names because they liked the sound of them. They chose names based on their meaning. Hacaliah's parents wanted their children to embody a truth they could cling to. I imagine Hacaliah's parents were living in exile in the Persian Empire, waiting on the Lord to do a great work, so when they had a son, they named him Hacaliah. They patiently waited for the Lord to do something great among his people, and this son of theirs did likewise.

Then Hacaliah grew up, got married, and established a family. He and his wife bore a son and named him Nehemiah, which means "the Lord comforts." Perhaps Hacaliah and his wife were comforted that God would continue their family line even though they lived in exile. Maybe there was hope that God would do something for his people, or possibly it went even deeper than that. By this point, the early waves of exiles had begun to return home. Perhaps Nehemiah's parents were comforted by the fact that they were witnessing God begin his work. Clearly, Nehemiah benefited from a godly lineage—godly parents and grandparents—who successfully instilled piety in him.

Grandparents and parents: Let Nehemiah's family history encourage you. Do the hard work of raising your kids in the nurture and admonition of the Lord, and make it your ambition to instill godliness in your kids. You cannot force it on them, but you can do everything possible to facilitate their spiritual growth. God may not call you personally to lead a great reformation of his people; however, you may be the one who trains the man or woman who leads a reformation. Or you may be like Hacaliah's parents—the couple that trains the father of the man who leads a reformation. You might be the link in a chain of godly people whom God uses to accomplish a great spiritual work. One such person was Nehemiah, the man God chose to complete the reformation of Israel, a man with a godly lineage whose family had instilled divine truths into his very soul.

In Nehemiah 1:11, we learn that he became a man of great importance in Babylon: *I was the cupbearer to the king.* As the name implies, a cupbearer's job was to bring food and drink to the king. Before the king ate or drank, the cupbearer would take a bite of the food and sip the wine. The king would then watch to see what happened. If the cupbearer enjoyed his meal, the king would eat. If the cupbearer grew sick or dropped dead, the king would know something was wrong. The cupbearer's job was to serve and protect the king. In time, though, the cupbearer's role became much more significant.

Because of their unique relationship, the cupbearer could become a confidant and an advisor to the king. It was truly a testament to Nehemiah's character that even though he was of a different ethnicity and a member of a conquered people, he would be the man whom the King of Persia would choose to stand by his side, to be his protector, to taste his food and drink, and to be his confidant and advisor. By the providence of God, Nehemiah was permitted to ascend to this great height. His social rank was also a testament to Nehemiah himself because he had earned the trust of the world's most powerful king. Nehemiah was the kind of person God could use to lead a reformation. He embraced the God of heaven as his king, had come to God in repentance and faith, and loved the Word of God and the people of God. However, Nehemiah was not content to see God's people in their beleaguered state. He wanted to be used by God to bring them back to full vitality, to bring God's Word back to the center of their lives. God can use this kind of man or woman.

IV. Reformation begins when that man understands the needs of the hour. How did this cupbearer in Persia become a leader of national reformation? Verse 1 tells us the exact moment it occurred: *It happened in the month of Chislev*, which was late fall on the Hebrew calendar. We also know the year it happened: *in the twentieth year*, the 20th year of the reign of Artaxerxes, the King of Persia, which places the events of this book at about 446 BC. Verse 1 even tells us where it happened: *I was in Susa, the capital.*

Susa was the winter retreat for the kings of Persia. When the weather started to turn, they would head there. The palace of Susa was one of the most incredible structures of the ancient world. Archaeologists discovered it in 1890, but it took them until 1960 to finish their excavations. In this compound, they found a beautiful, grand, central courtyard, a citadel, where the king hosted great feasts. Off to the side was another beautiful courtyard and a great apartment complex where the king's harem spent the winter.

On the opposite side of the compound was another series of grand courtyards with 80-foot-high pillars, gardens, statues, and marvels of every description. People waited in these courtyards if they wanted an audience with the king, and the courtyards were designed to fill these visitors with awe as they waited to speak to the king. In the center of this massive compound was the king's residence. At the top was his throne room, located above everything else so that he could see the entire estate and the horizon. The king and his court needed to climb a long, steep ramp to get to the throne room. The palace was an imposing structure.

So Nehemiah began with a godly lineage, grew up in exile in the Persian empire, and, in God's providence, was placed into the court of the most powerful man in the world. He rose to become the king's cupbearer, gained the king's ear, and became a confidant to the King of Persia. And because he was also a godly man, God was now ready to use him. In Verse 2, we learn that one day, while he was in Susa, Nehemiah was greeted by a delegation that included his brother Hanani. Nehemiah 7:2 says that Hanani was also a godly man. Nehemiah's whole family loved the Lord. Nehemiah 1:2 says Hanani came with certain men from Judah, far from Susa, so this delegation came a long way to speak with Nehemiah. They chose to speak to him because he was an Israelite like them, and they knew he had the ear of the king. They wanted Nehemiah to understand what was happening back in the Holy Land because they thought he was in a position to help.

After the delegation arrived at the Palace of Susa, Nehemiah asked about life in Israel. He inquired about the Jews who had escaped, those who had survived the exile, and about Jerusalem. Even though Nehemiah was living in the lap of luxury in the palace of a Persian king, his heart was still with the people of God. He could not help but ask, "How are things going back home? How are all the waves of exiles who had returned to Israel doing? Did they make it in one piece? Are they doing well? Have they established new homes? How are the families doing?" Nehemiah also wanted to know about the Jews who were not taken into captivity, the ones who had been left behind: "How have their grandchildren and great-grandchildren fared? Have they survived all this time?"

Finally, he inquired about Jerusalem because it was Israel's capital city, the center of politics, economics, and religious life. He asked, "How is the capital city? How is everything going back home?" He hoped for a good answer. Unfortunately, the answer was very sad. As we read in Verse 3, *They said to me, "The remnant there in the province who remain from the captivity are in great calamity and reproach."* Nehemiah had hoped for good news. He wanted to hear from his brother and the others that everybody was all together, safe and sound; they were rebuilding their lives and homes; the Temple was in place and the city restored; and God's people were alive and well. However, he heard the opposite: The situation was not good, even after 80 years since the first wave of exiles departed from Persia and returned to the Holy Land. God's people were still physically endangered and psychologically distressed. Why? The end of Verse 3 tells us: *Because the wall of Jerusalem is broken down and its gates are destroyed by fire.* Eighty years later, everything was still in shambles. The walls of Jerusalem still needed to be rebuilt.

Today, we must understand the importance of those walls. They were the only protection against foreign armies, marauders, and wild animals. To have no walls around a city meant its inhabitants were exposed to everything. The gates in those walls were important, too, because all of Jerusalem's legal and political matters were settled there. You might remember in the Book of Ruth how Boaz bargained with a relative at the city gates. Proverbs 31 speaks of the virtuous woman and how her husband met with the elders at the city gates. Gates were essential to a city's civic life, but the gates were still down in Jerusalem.

Those walls and gates also set up a cultural barrier between the Jewish people and their neighbors, helping to mark off the people of God from the rest. Inside those walls, God's people could worship him and follow the Scriptures without fear, but the whole city was still in ruins. Jerusalem's dilapidated state spoke to God's people's lack of spiritual resolve. Where was their zeal? Where was their passion to rebuild? Where was their desire to reconstitute their nation? The delegation that came to Susa brought terrible news to Nehemiah. After all these decades, the people of God were still a beleaguered group and spiritually depleted.

When you receive news like Nehemiah did, you can respond in several ways. You can react with indifference: "The city is still in shambles? Not my problem." Another way to respond is with sadness at the news but convincing yourself there is nothing you can do. In Nehemiah's case, he was many miles away from the problem. The King of Persia employed him, so it seemed unlikely that the king would let him leave. He could have said, "That is terrible news. It is awful, but what can I do?" But he did not. Another way to respond—the way Nehemiah responded—is to grieve as one should, but then resolve to act.

V. Resolve to act no matter the personal cost. Look at Nehemiah's response in Verse 4: *When I heard these words, I sat down and wept and mourned for days.* After hearing that the people of God were not doing well, that they were depressed, anxious, and vulnerable at a time when they should be thriving, Nehemiah responded correctly: He grieved. Because he was such a godly man, he grieved the bad news and then did something else: The Bible in Verse 4 says that he fasted for days. Fasting means going without food for some time to communicate that spiritual things are more important to you than food, so you go without food and pray to God instead. In your prayers, you say, "God, I have a problem on my hands, a massive spiritual problem, and it is more important than food. I do not need you to nourish my body right now. I need you to fix this spiritual calamity." That is what fasting is all about.

So Nehemiah wept, fasted, and prayed before the God of heaven. He begged God to do something: "God, you raised up King Cyrus already and sent your people back into the Holy Land. They have been there for decades now. Would you please revive your people and return them to their spiritual vitality? Help them to shake off their lethargy." Toward the end of his prayers, perhaps he said, "God, show me how I can help. Use me to bring reformation to your people." Later in the book, we will learn that God answered Nehemiah's prayer, and Nehemiah would soon leave his comfortable life in the Persian palace to live in the ash heap of Jerusalem. Why? Because this is what godly leaders do. When they see a spiritual need, they act, sparking reformations. They rise up and build, not for their own glory but to make a name for God. What breaks the heart of a godly leader is to see God's people in shambles because it means God's reputation is being harmed and his name is not being exalted. It also breaks the heart of godly leaders to see God's people in a spiritually low state because they know what it means for God himself.

A leader like Nehemiah will rise up for God's glory, help his people rebuild, and give God the glory from beginning to end. We will see this "resolve to act" as we work together through the book. Nehemiah 1:10 speaks of the Israelites as *a people redeemed by God*. Nehemiah 2:8 talks about his work promoting a national rebirth when he says, *The good hand of my God was on me*. Nehemiah 2:18 speaks about the work being done and that God is working among them for the people's good. Nehemiah 4:15 states that, as the Israelites began to experience opposition in the work, *God had thwarted their counsel* or hindered the opposition's plans. And then, in Nehemiah 7:5, when an important idea came to him, Nehemiah writes, *God put it into my heart*. Throughout this effort, Nehemiah refers to himself and his co-laborers as God's servants. He does not try to rebuild the nation for his own glory. He does it for God's glory. God will get all the credit for it from beginning to end.

VI. Application. Friends, do you want to be used by God to spark a reformation in your own day? Do you want God to use you, your children, or your grandchildren to bring about that reformation? Then, strive to become the kind of man or woman that God can use to bring about such a reformation. Let it begin with you. Be sure you have come to God in repentance and faith and are rightly related to him. Then, engage in the work necessary to grow in godliness. Study the Bible daily and then gather with God's people weekly to study the Scriptures further. Take every opportunity to attend a Bible study, a Sunday school class, or a worship service. Learn how to apply God's Word to your life. Fill your life with it, and let God use it to prompt you to act. Let a zeal for God's cause begin to stir within you.

Parents and grandparents: Make it your mission to raise your children and grandchildren in the nurture and admonition of the Lord. Perhaps if God does not use you to spark a great reformation, he will use your child or grandchild. Let it begin with you. Seek to understand the needs of the hour. Look at yourself. Look at the state of God's people and Christ's Church today, and then ask yourself, "Where are the battles being fought right now? Where are the theological controversies raging? What is the Church's greatest point of weakness? Where is she failing? Where is the Church becoming demoralized and discouraged? Where is the Church showing a loss of confidence in the Word of God?" Ask yourself what would bring her back to vitality: "What action must be taken? What words must be spoken? What books must be published? What prayers need to be offered? What must be done?" And friend, resolve to act once you have answered these questions. Do not say the problem is too great or think God cannot use a person like you. No, take it upon yourself to do what you can with the resources God has given you, looking at where God has placed you in his providence.

Be the first to act, but realize it will cost you time, money, and effort. There will be a season of preparation like there was for Nehemiah, but then you must roll up your sleeves and get to work. There will be times when you will grow fatigued because of the work. Emotionally and physically, you might feel spent. There may be a cost in friendships or reputation as you wholly give yourself to this work. There will be controversy as you pick a side and then argue forcefully for it while working to build the institutions supporting it as you seek a revival. When you plant your flag on one side, the other side will react. There will be a cost. It will come with adversity, but by his grace, God can use you to bring reform to his people. He can use you in your sphere of influence, and perhaps, as you are faithful there, he will give you greater platforms to instill in others the confidence they can find in his Word. God can use you to spark a reawakening of spiritual concern. He can use you to strengthen what remains and then build and go on the offense. He can use you to accomplish the biblical mission, and he can do it now in our generation.

VII. Conclusion. We live in times when the Church in America has lost its confidence in the Word of God. It resorts to tricks and gimmicks to draw people into its services because it lacks confidence in the Gospel's power to transform lives. Very few serious churches remain today. How can a reformation begin? It will start when God moves upon an individual who understands the needs of the hour and is willing to act, no matter the personal cost. My friends, let this reformation begin with us.

Chapter Two

REBUILDING OUR PRAYER LIVES

The first action of a godly reformer is to pray.

I. Introduction to sermon on Nehemiah 1:5-11. Many of you know Martin Luther, who was born in Germany in 1483. As he grew up, he thought he would pursue a career in law. But one day in young adulthood, while walking home late at night, he got caught in a thunderstorm. Suddenly, a giant bolt of lightning struck right in front of him, and he went into a panic. In his panic, he prayed to Saint Anne and said, "I will become a monk if you spare me tonight." Of course, his life was spared, and he kept his vow. Luther became a Catholic monk. He put his heart and soul into that work and fasted more than anybody else. He denied himself sleep and went on pilgrimages. Everything Luther could do as a monk, he did. And what he was trying to do was earn a place in heaven. He thought that if he did enough good works, God would see him as a righteous man and welcome him into the gates of heaven.

Eventually, Martin Luther was appointed as a professor of theology at the University of Wittenberg. As he began to prepare for his classes, he studied the Book of Psalms and then went to the Book of Romans. His study of Romans changed his life. When he came to Romans 3:21-26, here was what he read: *But now apart from the Law the righteousness of God has been manifested, being witnessed by the Law and the Prophets, even the righteousness of God through faith in Jesus Christ for all those who believe; for there is no distinction; for all have sinned and fall short of the glory of God, being justified as a gift by his grace through the redemption which is in Christ Jesus; whom God displayed publicly as a propitiation in his blood through faith, for a demonstration of his righteousness, because in the forbearance of God he passed over the sins previously committed; for the demonstration of his righteousness at present, so that he would be just and the justifier of the one who has faith in Jesus.* This passage showed God's righteousness at present so that he might be just and the justifier of the one who has faith in Jesus.

As Luther read these words, the scales of spiritual blindness fell from his eyes, and he realized that his entire life pursuit had all been a waste. He discovered that we cannot be made righteous in God's sight. Instead, we must be declared righteous through Christ's imputed righteousness. In other words, a righteous standing before God is not something we earn; it is a gift we receive from God by faith alone, trusting in the all-sufficiency of Christ's righteousness and his atoning sacrifice for our sins. Martin Luther finally came to that understanding. He was born again and became a new creation in Christ. His whole life changed.

At about the same time Luther underwent this transformation, the Pope in Rome renewed a building project. He wanted to finish St. Peter's Basilica, the massive church where he resided, so he sent representatives all over Europe to start raising funds. He offered an incentive to anybody who would give money for the project, and gave his representatives little slips of paper called indulgences, which provided the forgiveness of sins, as provided by the Pope. The Vatican's representatives went into all the towns, villages, and hamlets throughout Europe and offered these slips of paper, along with the following message: "Give us money to finish the building project and, in exchange, we will give you these slips of paper forgiving your sins."

It was a horrific program: Give money and receive forgiveness. The medieval Catholic Church raked in an enormous amount of money through this program. In Martin Luther's neck of the woods, one particularly effective salesman named Johann Tetzel, went through the process and came up with a sales jingle, which went something like this: "As soon as a coin in the coffer rings / the soul from purgatory spring." In other words, "Give me your money; if you do, you can get your loved ones out of purgatory." So these indulgences were used not just for oneself but also for people's loved ones. Tetzel made a fortune with his jingle.

When Luther, this now-born-again Christian, saw what was happening, his heart broke because he understood that salvation is a gift from God. The only thing required was to receive it by faith, so the thought that a church would tell people to perform good works or give money for forgiveness and salvation left him heartbroken. Because he was a scholarly man, he responded by taking a pen and paper and writing out why indulgences were wrong. He came up with 95 reasons, which became known as his 95 Theses. He wrote them all down, explaining that salvation was a gift of God that you could neither earn nor buy. He then posted his 95 Theses on the door of Castle Church in Wittenberg, Germany, which functioned as the public bulletin board in that day. He meant to start a public debate.

The church, however, reacted violently to the 95 Theses. Luther faced heresy charges and eventually was excommunicated from the church. Of course, he famously took his excommunication papers and burned them at a public ceremony. Historically, Martin Luther posted those 95 theses on October 31, 1517. Our culture celebrates Halloween on that night, but Christians know it as Reformation Day. The posting of those 95 theses marked the symbolic beginning of the Protestant Reformation. The Lutheran Church began as a renewal movement within the medieval Catholic Church. However, it soon became a new, separated church.

First, the Lutheran Church was named after Martin Luther, who hated that the church was named after him. He said, "The church belongs to Christ, not to me." But it remained the Lutheran Church. Later, the Reformed Church, its various branches, and the Free Church tradition would emerge. Through one man's action, a new spiritual movement changed the course of an entire generation, and that generation impacted all subsequent generations. Today, our church is heir to that 16th-century reformation. Many of us remember Martin Luther for his brave actions: his public speeches, the 95 Theses, the books he wrote, the debates he engaged in, and his burning of the excommunication papers. We also remember his commentary on the Book of Romans and the church he founded, which still bears his name.

What he is not as well remembered for but should be remembered for is that he was also a man of prayer. On one occasion, he said, "As is the business of tailors to make clothes and cobblers to make shoes, so it is the business of Christians to pray." One of my favorite quotes from Martin Luther occurred when he was heading into a very busy day. Either in conversation or with somebody overhearing him, he was quoted as saying, "Work, work from early until late. In fact, I have so much to do that I shall spend the first three hours in prayer." For Martin Luther, a busy schedule was not an excuse to neglect prayer. Rather, the busier he got, the more he felt he needed to pray. He understood that his project, this Reformation project, would ultimately be a work of God, so if it had any lasting effect, God would need to be the primary mover. Every day, he bathed his work in prayer.

Friends, today we are back in the Book of Nehemiah, a book about reformation. It describes how God used Nehemiah to complete the national reformation of Israel in his day. We began this series last week and asked the question, "How does a reformation begin?" Here is the answer: Reformation can start when a man of God, understanding the needs of the hour, resolves to act no matter the personal cost. I will repeat that answer. Reformation can begin when a man of God, who understands the needs of the hour, resolves to act no matter the personal cost. It is just as simple as that. God can spark a reformation with just one person: someone who has been transformed by his grace, who is possessed by a love for God and his people, who has reforming zeal, and who wants to see God do something great in this current generation. Such a person wants to see people come to faith in God, as well as see those already believing in God renewed and reformed by his Word. It takes just one person who wants to be used by God to start a movement that will spark reform in a whole generation, creating a ripple effect on all generations.

We now will advance to Nehemiah 1:5-11 and ask the following question: What is the first action a reformer should take? Of course, the answer is prayer, and not just a short, casual kind of prayer that you tack on to your morning devotions. It requires real, time-consuming, energy-burning prayer for God to do a work in your generation—a work of reformation and revival. It takes prayer to get it started.

II. What is prayer? Why is prayer important? Simply put, prayer is communicating to God all of the righteous desires of your heart with the expectation that he will hear you and respond to you. Why is prayer important? Because, ultimately, reformation is a work of God, so if anything is going to happen, it will require God moving among his people. The exciting part is that God promises to use our prayers to accomplish his purposes. Do you want to see the people of God in your generation reformed by the Word of God? Do you want to see the Gospel spreading out into new territory? Do you want to see the Church of Christ on the offensive for a change instead of being on defense? Then you must pray for it—fervently—and start your work with prayer, believing that God will use your prayers to do his good work. Matthew 7:7 says, *"Ask, and it will be given to you; seek, and you will find; knock, and it* *will be opened to you."* Matthew 21:22 says, *"And all things you ask in prayer, believing, you will receive."* James 5:16 says, *The effective prayer of a righteous man can accomplish much.*

I love this quote from Pastor E. M. Bounds, who wrote that prayer "is a voice which goes into God's ear, and it lives as long as God's ear is open to holy pleas, as long as God's heart is alive to holy things" which, is to say, it lives forever. Here are some other quotes from Bounds:

- "When God's house on earth is a house of prayer, then God's house in heaven is busy and all potent in its plans and movements."
- "The more praying there is in the world the better the world will be, the mightier the forces against evil everywhere."
- "Prayer puts God in full force in the world. To a prayerful man God is present in realised force."
- "The one who can wield the power of prayer is the strong one, the holy one in Christ's Kingdom."
- "They [those who pray] are God's heroes, God's saints, God's servants, God's vicegerents [or agents]."

Friends, if we want God to perform a new work in our generation, revive his people and reform them by his Word, if we want to see the Gospel reach new territory in our generation, we will need to pray. We must believe God's promises that he will start a work among us if we pray in faith.

III. How should a reformer pray? How should a reformer pray, and what form should a reformer's prayers take? Today's text shows us the way. As soon as Nehemiah realized the need to confront God's people in his day, he immediately fell to his knees and began praying. Here in these verses, we have a record of Nehemiah's prayers, which consists of five parts. Let us quickly work through these parts and use them as a model for our prayer lives as we seek reformation.

First, Nehemiah invoked God's name in Verse 5: *I said, "I beseech You, O Yahweh, the God of heaven, the great and fearsome God."* He began his prayer by addressing God like we would in conversation. If you want my attention, you would say, "Pastor Brandon, come here." That would get my attention. We should do the same in prayer: Call to God by name. Here in Verse 5,

Nehemiah used a compound name for God, calling him the *God of heaven*. In some translations, the word LORD is in all caps, which translates the Hebrew name *Yahweh*. It means "I am" and speaks to God's infinite nature. God dwells in the eternal present, has always existed, and will always exist. He is self-existing, self-sustaining, and self-revealing. Nehemiah then called him *the God of heaven*. These words contrasted the God he was praying to with all the gods the Persians worshipped. Theirs were gods of the earth, wood, stone, and men's imaginations. But Nehemiah said, "No, my God is *the God of heaven*. He dwells above the earth. He is enthroned above the stars."

Both of these names that Nehemiah used are ones that God had revealed to man. God also claimed them as his name: I am *Yahweh*, the "I am." I am the true and living God, *the God of Heaven*. We should follow Nehemiah's example when we pray to God for reformation. Begin your prayer by invoking God's name, the ones he has revealed to us in the Scriptures—names that speak to his power, sovereignty, infinite nature, and ability to do anything we ask of him. Notice that Nehemiah did not take a casual approach to God's name like many church leaders do today. He did not call him "Daddy" or "Hey God." God is not deserving of that. He deserves our highest reverence. Nehemiah talked to God with a spirit of absolute reverence, calling him the *I am, the God of Heaven*. Friends, let us have an extensive view of God. Speak to him with the honor he is due. God would be pleased with a prayer that begins like that.

Now we move on to the next part of Nehemiah's prayer: He exalted God's attributes. In Verse 5, he called God by name and delighted in his attributes: *O Yahweh, the God of heaven, the great and fearsome God.* The word translated as *great* here means "big and strong." God is omnipotent—the God who can do anything, the God who will not falter no matter how big your request is. He can answer any prayer if it aligns with his will, not just yours. He is great and awesome, which means he is awe-inspiring. In the Scriptures, when even the holiest men get the slightest glimpse of God's glory, what do they do? Immediately, they fall on their faces like dead men. God's awe-inspiring attributes and works leave his people wide-eyed and slack-jawed, falling on their faces before him. He is a great God. Notice that Nehemiah moved next to God's moral attributes: He is excellent and good, and *"the great and fearsome God, who keeps the covenant and lovingkindness for those who love Him and keep His commandments."* He is the faithful God, the trustworthy God, the God who loves his people. And that love never wavers.

Nehemiah was probably also thinking about Israel's national covenant with God here. God had pledged himself to Israel, and the people of Israel had pledged themselves back to God, but now they had failed, forsaking every part of their covenant. But God had been faithful to every single letter. He is faithful, great, and good—all of which is to say God is holy and separate from and above the world that he made. We are the creatures. He is the creator. We are finite. He is infinite. We are sinful. He is sinless. God is in a category all to himself. Friends, if reformation is ever to take hold of the American Church, I believe it will begin with a new appreciation for God's holiness, seeing him for who he truly is. We must pray to him, invoking his names in reverence and delighting in his holiness. I believe that getting a new sense of God's holiness will also drive us to confess our sins, which is necessary if reformation is to take hold. This sense of holiness is just what Nehemiah did next.

Look at Nehemiah 1:6 with me: *Let Your ear now be attentive and Your eyes open to hear the prayer of Your slave which I am praying before You today, day and night, on behalf of the sons of Israel Your slaves.* Nehemiah invoked God's name and worshipped him for his greatness and goodness. Then he pleaded with him: "God, please incline yourself to me. Hear my requests." Then, he began confessing sins, saying, "Listen to me," *confessing the sins of the sons of Israel which we have sinned against You; I and my father's house have sinned.* Notice a three-part confession here.

First, he confessed the sinfulness of his nation, *the sins of the sons of Israel*, and indeed, their sins were great. I have already mentioned that they violated every covenant term with God. They were supposed to love God with all their heart, soul, mind, and strength, but they had no love for God at all. They paid him lip service, but their hearts were far from him. They chased after other gods. They worshipped idols and went so far as to sacrifice their children to placate their idols. That was how far they had fallen. If a national revival and reformation were to take hold, it would need to start with them confessing their sins: "God, forgive us for what we have done. Forgive us for our unfaithfulness to you."

Then, notice the second part of his confession: He included himself in that sin formation. He said *We have sinned against You.* Nehemiah was an Israelite, so he was a part of this corporate body. Nehemiah did not stand apart from the Israelites, saying "they" need forgiveness; "they" are really bad. No. He said, "God, I am one of them. We are all sinners against you. We all need your grace." In the third part, he personalized his confession, saying *I and my father's house have sinned.* Not only did he admit that he was part of a corporate body that had failed God, but he also confessed that he and his household had participated in the nation's sinfulness. They were all sinners before God.

What is sin? John Piper defines it this way: Sin "is the glory of God not honored. The holiness of God not reverenced. The greatness of God not admired. The power of God not praised. The truth of God not sought. The wisdom of God not esteemed. The beauty of God not treasured. The goodness of God not savored. The faithfulness of God not trusted. The commandments of God not obeyed. The justice of God not respected. The wrath of God not feared. The grace of God not cherished. The presence of God not prized. The person of God not loved. That is sin."

When we do not regard the greatest of all beings, the one who makes us, loves us, and offers us his very salvation and his very life, and when we look at him as no one of great importance and spend our lives chasing after lesser things, that is sin. It is our failure toward God. And we are all implicated in this. Nehemiah was right to include himself. Romans 3:23 says, *For all have sinned and fall short of the glory of God*. Romans 6:23 explains the consequences: *The wages of sin is death* or an eternal separation from God. Sin is why the Israelites were driven into exile—not because God had been unfaithful to them but because they had been unfaithful to God. They made promises to God who, in turn, made promises to them. God kept his promises. They broke theirs, and the consequences were a lost monarchy, a lost temple, a lost capital city, and a lost land. They were scattered into exile and thrown to the four winds of pagan empires. Their sins were great. They needed to confess them, be forgiven, and thus be reconciled to God.

Friends, reformation cannot begin until we acknowledge a difficult truth about ourselves: God is holy, but we are not. The pain and suffering we endure in life are not God's fault. We live in a sin-cursed world and thus need to call out to God as the solution to our problems, not as the cause of them. As the leader of God's people in his day, Nehemiah came to God on behalf of all Israelites, confessing their sins. Christian, are there sins you should confess today and talk to God about? Are there sins you have been hiding from others but God knows are there? Perhaps you are the head of a household, and there may be family sins that must be confessed. Church leaders, perhaps congregational sins need to be taken to the throne of grace for God's forgiveness. Only then will the Church be ready for a reformation to take hold.

Nehemiah spearheaded reformation in this way: He invoked God's name, delighted in God's attributes, and immediately confessed sin. In Nehemiah 1:8-9 we see that he offered his righteous requests in a quote from Deuteronomy 30: *Remember the word which You commanded Your servant Moses,* saying, "*If you are unfaithful, I will scatter you among the peoples; but if you return to Me and keep My commandments and do them, though those of you who have been banished were at the ends of the sky, I will gather them from there and will bring them to the place where I have chosen to cause My name to dwell."* Nehemiah prayed for God's promises.

When Israel made this national covenant with God, the covenant said that if the people were faithful, they would remain in their land and enjoy prosperity. They would lose everything and be scattered to the four winds if unfaithful. Well, they had been unfaithful, and now they were in exile. So, Nehemiah was asking God to fulfill his promise to restore them: "God, in Your Word, You say that if Your people confess their sins, You will reconcile with them. You will bring them back into their land. You will be their God again. They will be Your people." He also said, "God, we have done that now. I have prayed to you. I have confessed our sins. I know we are guilty. I have asked you to forgive us. So now, will you fulfill your promise, God? Will you restore us now? Will you do a new work among us?"

Friends, we can pray for the promises of God, too. It is good for us to come to God with our own words, but it is also good for us to go with the words of God himself. We can pray to him, saying "God, in your Word, we declare that this is your will for your Church and your people. Here are the promises that you have made. I now ask you to fulfill your Word. Please answer this prayer and fulfill your promise. God, in my sight, let me witness you fulfilling your own words." I believe God would be pleased to answer a prayer like that if we pray it with reverence and faith.

Nehemiah 1:10 adds a further motivation for God to act when he says in Verse 10, *They are Your slaves and Your people whom You redeemed by Your great power and by Your strong hand.* He said, "God, do not forget who these people are. They were slaves in Egypt long ago, but you rescued them, saved them, and made them your own. Do not forget the special relationship that you have with these people. God, let that motivate you to save them again." Friends, it is good for us to do the same as we pray to God. We can delight in all of his past work in our lives. Individually, in our families, and as a congregation, we can remember the good works of God and say, "God, renew your works among us. Do not forsake your people."

Finally, Nehemiah prayed for success, which forms the final part of his prayer in Verse 11: *O Lord, I beseech You, may Your ear be attentive to the prayer of Your slave and the prayer of Your slaves who delight to fear Your name, and make Your slave successful today and grant him compassion before this man.* This man was King Artaxerxes, Nehemiah's boss. You see, Nehemiah was about to get up off his knees, march into the throne room of the most powerful man in the world, and ask the king to let him leave his job as cupbearer so he could take the long trek to the Holy Land and help complete the reformation of God's people in Israel. And then he concluded his prayer with God: "Please give me success. Let me have a part in the reformation of your people."

IV. Summary. Friends, we have seen that the first action a godly leader must take if he desires reformation is to pray. If anything great is to be accomplished, it can only be done through the power of prayer. How often do we think of prayer as the least productive thing we can do with our time when, in truth, it may be the most productive? And so, friends, let us learn how to pray. Let us set aside a portion of each day to engage God in prayer and follow the pattern exemplified in Nehemiah's prayer. Begin by addressing God by name, the names he has revealed in Scripture. Then, exult in God's attributes, offer your requests, confess your sins, plead his promises, ask for success, and pray like Nehemiah did.

V. Conclusion. What should a Godly reformer do after praying or, perhaps, while praying? He should roll up his sleeves and put his feet to those prayers. Nehemiah's final request was to ask God to grant him mercy in the sight of King Artaxerxes. He prayed for reformation, but he also wanted to be a part of it. We pray, and then we get to work; we get off our knees and get on our feet.

Chapter Three

REBUILDING OUR MORAL COURAGE

GODLY REFORMERS HAVE MORAL COURAGE.

I. Introduction to sermon on Nehemiah 2:1-8. I opened last week's message with a story about Martin Luther. Today, we begin with a story about John Calvin. He was a Frenchman born in 1509. His parents immediately realized they had a prodigy on their hands. He was so clever that, by age 14, he had been accepted into the most prestigious university in Europe, the University of Paris. Calvin earned his Bachelor of Theology and then his Master of Theology there, completing both degrees when he was 19. He then transferred to another university to pursue a Master's degree in Law. By age 23, he had earned two Master's degrees: one in Theology and one in Law.

While studying for his law degree, he encountered the writings of Martin Luther, who was about 25 years older. Luther had been pursuing reform in Germany for as long as Calvin had been alive. He compared Luther's writings with the Scriptures and realized Luther was right. Up to this point, Calvin had held the conviction that a man was saved by grace, through faith, plus works. He maintained that Christ's atoning work was only a partial atonement, that Christ supplied part of what we needed to be justified in the sight of God, but that we had to supply the other part through our good works. By combining

Christ's work with ours, he believed we would earn a righteous standing with God. This was the doctrine that young Calvin once embraced.

But then he studied Luther. From there, he went to the Scriptures and learned that a righteous standing before God was not something we could earn, not in whole or part. It is a gift from God, given to us when we repent of our sins and believe in Jesus Christ. Calvin understood this in his early twenties and thus was born again. Immediately afterward, he threw himself into reforming the Church in France. Because of his intellectual gifts, he began working as a speech writer. At that time, France was a Roman Catholic country, so the persecution was very hard against Protestant reformers like Calvin. He was forced to flee France and go to Switzerland. There, he commenced a life of scholarship and began writing the book that would make him most famous, *The Institutes of the Christian Religion*, a theology textbook and one of the most influential works of theology in the church's history. It is still in print today. He published the first edition at 26 and then traveled from Switzerland to Strasbourg, Germany, where he would conduct additional research and writing. However, the journey took him through the city of Geneva, which, at the time, was about the size of our city and located at the border of Switzerland and France.

As soon as he entered Geneva, the town residents recognized him as the author of *The Institutes*. They were so excited to see Calvin in their city that they ran up to him and said, "You have got to meet our leader, William Farrel." For the last ten years, Farrel had been pursuing the reformation of the Church of Geneva, so they introduced Calvin to him. Immediately, Farrel realized he had met the man Geneva needed. Farrel was zealous about bringing the Protestant Reformation to Geneva. However, he had a harsh personality and tended to rub people the wrong way. He also lacked Calvin's intellectual gifts and knew he could only take this reformation so far, so he presented the following proposal: "Calvin, I want to hand the reins of leadership over to you. I want you to become the pastor of the Church of Geneva and complete this reformation for us."

Calvin replied, "No, you do not understand. I am not a people person. Pastors need to be people persons. The only thing I am suited for is scholarship, so the best way to serve the reformation is to lock myself away and read and write books. That is what I am called to do." Farrel was furious at Calvin's reply, so he uttered a curse on Calvin, saying, "May God curse all of your labors. May he give you no health. May he give you no sleep. May all of your scholarly works be a miserable failure. May all your teeth fall out. May you get bed bugs." (I am making some of this up, but you all understand.)

These imprecations scared Calvin, so he changed his mind and became the pastor of the Church in Geneva. The first thing he did was begin preaching expositionally through the Scriptures. He began with a book of the Bible and systematically preached through it one passage at a time. As he went through the Scriptures in this manner, he taught people the content of Scripture and the doctrines that derived from it. As the congregation learned the Scriptures, he began implementing necessary church reforms. This process was hard work and required much patience. There was much opposition, but Calvin pursued his reformation slowly and steadily.

However, his reforms finally came to a head on Easter Sunday of 1538, when he began practicing church discipline. Several prominent members of the church were not born again, and they showed no evidence of love for God or his people. Their lives were scandalous, so Calvin excommunicated them, which excluded them from receiving communion, the mark of church membership. Furious at their excommunication, these prominent Geneva citizens and church members went straight to the city council in Geneva, which summoned Calvin to appear before them. They said, "You must reinstate these men to membership. If you do not, you are gone. You are fired. Leave town." That was the state of their church at that time: The City Council decided who was a church member and who was not. They determined who would serve as pastor because they paid the pastor's salary.

This ultimatum confronted Calvin with a genuine crisis. He truly believed that (a) the well-being of the Church was at stake here, (b) Christ was the head of the Church, not the Geneva City Council, (c) Christ clearly stated in his Word who was qualified for Church membership, and (d) Christ had entrusted to the elders of the church (not city council members) who should be in as members and who should be out. Calvin was firmly convinced about these truths but realized he could lose everything if he stood firm—his job, home, and who knows what else—but he decided that this situation was a hill worth dying on. Christ would be the head of the Church in Geneva.

The elders that Christ had established in this church would decide who would receive communion and who would not. The Church would no longer be corrupted by a city council that did not understand the Scriptures. He looked those city council members in the eye and said, "I will not comply with your orders. I will not reinstate these men to membership." Of course, Calvin was fired and run out of town. He fled to Germany. I wish I had time to give you the rest of the details of his life. However, three years after his exile from Geneva, the City Council contacted Calvin by letter, saying, "We need you to come back. Since you left, the city has fallen apart. The Church has fallen apart. You are the only man who can turn this thing around. We are willing to follow your program now." Calvin received that letter and responded, "No way. I would rather die a hundred deaths than go back to Geneva. If I go back, I will have to die a thousand deaths every day." But six months later, he changed his mind. He returned to Geneva and spent the next 25 years of his life laboring for the church's reformation there. It was difficult, and he faced much opposition, but he stuck with it until his death.

The Lord used John Calvin and the other elders of that church to do some incredible things. During his tenure there, Calvin completed a commentary on the Bible, which is still in print today, and he helped facilitate the *Geneva Study Bible*, the world's first study Bible. Calvin also established a school called the Geneva Academy. Most remarkable of all, the Church of Geneva, during those 25 years of Calvin's tenure, sent out 1,300 missionaries who spread all over Europe and established gospel churches as far as South America. Millions today owe a debt to Calvin's ministry. Calvin finally passed away on May 27, 1564, at 54.

Friends, John Calvin is a profile in moral courage. What is moral courage? Rosabeth Kanter of Harvard says, "Moral courage enables people to stand up for a principle rather than stand on the sidelines." Another writer, Aarne P. Vesilind, states, "Moral courage is the courage to take principled action even at the risk of adverse consequences." Many people believe that moral courage is the most essential quality of leadership. After all, if you do not have a moral core, what do you stand for? What are you leading people to do without a moral core? It is the most important thing about a leader, and it is a critical virtue for anyone whom God would use to bring reformation to his people.

As we return to the Book of Nehemiah today, we find that Nehemiah was a leader with moral courage. If you are joining us for the first time, we have been in this series, looking at Nehemiah, the cupbearer to King Artaxerxes in Persia many centuries ago. He was also an Israelite with a love for God and a heart for his people. We have been looking at how God used him and a small handful of others to complete the reformation of his people in Israel. By studying Nehemiah's story, we have been learning about the principles of a godly reformer and what drives a godly reformer to do his work. We hope to apply these principles to our lives so that God might even use us and our church to bring scriptural reform to the people of God today.

As a congregation, we have already discovered several important principles from this book. Last week, we learned that godly reformers are people of prayer. If reformation is to take hold, it will be a work of God, a spiritual work, so we pray to God to work in our hearts and raise up leaders so there will be a new appreciation for God's Word, a new desire in our will to bend to God's Word and a new zeal for his cause. Godly reformers are people of prayer. Today's text will teach us this truth: Godly reformers are also people of moral courage. They are willing to take a principled stand, even when danger is involved.

II. Moral courage means feeling the weight of a moral crisis. Let us look at Nehemiah 2:1-8, beginning with the first verse: *Now I had not been sad in his presence.* That is, not until now. Looking back at the first statement of Verse 1, we are *in the month of Nisan*, which is springtime on our calendar. It had been about four months since Nehemiah first heard the awful news about the state of God's people in Israel. Remember, the Israelites had been exiled in pagan empires for generations, but for the past 80 years, God had been bringing them back into the Holy Land in various waves. Nehemiah, the cupbearer to the King of Persia, was one of those Israelites who remained in exile.

One day, Nehemiah heard from his brother and a contingent of men from the Holy Land that all was not going well for the people in Jerusalem. Their temple repairs needed to be completed, and the capital city was still in ruins. Depressed and beleaguered, the people of God were at a spiritual low. Because of this awful news, Nehemiah cried, fasted, prayed, and began thinking about what God might do to turn this situation around and use him to lead a reformation, to spark a revival of the people. Finally, Nehemiah decided that he was in a position to help God's people, so he chose a day when he would make his first move, and that is what we see here in Verse 1, which sets the stage for the entire scene.

Four months had passed since his decision, and the day had finally come. It was a lot like any other day in Nehemiah's life. He was standing beside the King, as he always did, bringing a goblet of wine into his presence. Nehemiah took the goblet, sampled a drink from the wine to ensure it was not poisoned, and then handed it to King Artaxerxes. But something was different on this occasion. We read about it at the end of Verse 1: Nehemiah allowed himself to appear sad in the King's presence. He allowed all of the grief he had been feeling for the past four months to finally express itself on his face.

Why did Nehemiah do this? Because there were rules about servants and kings in those days, a servant could not strike up a conversation with his king. Nehemiah could not just walk into the King's throne room and say, "Hey, King, I have this problem. There is all of this trouble in the Holy Land. The people of God are beleaguered." He needed King Artaxerxes to initiate the conversation, but how would that happen? Well, Nehemiah came up with an idea. After four months of praying and thinking about it, he decided to present himself before the King and allow him to see his grief, which was a breach of protocol. You do not bring your problems into the King's presence, but it was a minor breach, so he did it.

Verse 2 shows that the plan worked: *So the king said to me, "Why is your face sad though you are not sick?"* Artaxerxes noticed that Nehemiah appeared sad. The word translated "sad" here means "overcome with sorrow." Nehemiah was overcome. The King asked, *Why is your face sad, though you are not sick? This is nothing but sadness of heart.* He essentially said, "Nehemiah, you look terrible." This scene reminds me of what some of Abraham Lincoln's cabinet members said about the president during the Civil War. They said they had never seen a sadder face in their lives than the face of Abraham Lincoln.

I imagine that is what King Artaxerxes thought as he looked at Nehemiah. That is the saddest face I have ever seen. And so he said to Nehemiah, "Why are you so sad? You are not sick. You must be heartsick. What is wrong with your heart?" Artaxerxes was exactly right. Nehemiah was heartsick. He was completely woebegone, and his heart was bleeding for the people of God. For 80 years, God's people had been moving back into the Holy Land. By now, Israel should be thriving, the Temple should be up and filled with worshippers, the city walls should be built, Jerusalem should be a thriving metropolis, and God's people should be like a city on a hill. However, none of that had happened. Nehemiah was heartsick.

Friends, if you want to be a leader with moral courage, you must be able to feel the weight of a moral crisis, which is what we see in Nehemiah. How does that happen? How does that weight come upon us? It happens when we have developed our moral core for truths, virtues, and causes that we cling to. When the idea of losing something or someone dear to you is too much to bear, you must become the kind of leader that is needed. Nehemiah loved God, wanted to see God's cause advance in the world, and loved the people of God. He wanted to see them accomplish God's mission, but in their current state, it was not happening, which caused Nehemiah's heart to break. However, this heartbreak motivated him to act. The people and place he most valued in the world were under threat, and he needed to remedy this. Friend, a firm moral core will also help you become a leader with moral courage. When you see the things you value crumbling around you, you cannot help but stand up and do something.

III. Overcoming the fears that lead to paralysis. Nehemiah 2:2 indicates that King Artaxerxes saw sadness on Nehemiah's face and responded that Nehemiah must be heartsick. The cupbearer had been waiting for this moment. He finally got to talk to the King about the problem after praying for it and planning how he would do it. But now, the moment finally arrived, and notice what he says: *Then I was very much afraid*. Here, we see Nehemiah's humanity. Yes, he is a man of God and has been praying and planning for four months, but when the moment finally arrived, and he had to open his mouth and speak to the most powerful man in the world, he was scared to death.

Why was he so frightened? Well, friends, the story has a wrinkle that we still need to discuss. Jerusalem was still in ruins because King Artaxerxes had decreed that construction on the city should stop, which we learn about in Ezra 4. Some advisors had come to Artaxerxes while the city was being rebuilt, and they said, "Hey, Artaxerxes, do you not realize Jerusalem's reputation? This city has always been a seedbed for rebellion. Jerusalem rises and fights back whenever an empire occupies the Holy Land. You do not want that to happen to you, do you? You must stop the rebuilding." This is why Nehemiah was scared.

The Holy Land needed to be rebuilt, and God's people needed their temple and capital city restored. Yet, Nehemiah's boss was the one who brought it all to a stop and did not allow the construction to continue. How would King Artaxerxes respond if Nehemiah said, "We must rebuild that city." How would the King take this? Remember, Nehemiah was also an Israelite—a foreigner. So, if this Israelite cupbearer insisted we needed to rebuild Israel, would King Artaxerxes think that Nehemiah was trying to foment rebellion as part of some insurrectionist group? Would Nehemiah be imprisoned or killed? All these thoughts must have been going through Nehemiah's head as he began speaking to Artaxerxes.

Yet, as great as his fear was, he would not allow that fear to control him because he believed Jerusalem needed to be rebuilt. God's people could not be revived until their institutions, including the Temple and the capital city, were restored. As frightened as Nehemiah was, he would keep addressing the issue. This is what moral courage is all about: conviction conquering fear. Having moral courage means feeling the weight of the moral crisis and overcoming any fears that lead to inaction.

IV. Boldly pursuing a wise course of action. In Nehemiah 2:3-8, we read that moral courage means boldly pursuing a wise course of action, which includes speaking respectfully and clearly to those people who created the crisis. Look at Verse 3 with me, where Nehemiah writes, *I said to the king, "Let the king live forever."* He began his conversation with the King in a way that communicated his love for Artaxerxes: "So, Artaxerxes, I am about to tell you something very difficult for me to discuss. There is a chance you will take this wrong, but I want you to know before I say anything else that I love you and value your kingship. I hope you live a long time. I want your kingdom to thrive. Yet, I have to address a problem." He then moved on with the heart of his message: *"Why should my face not be sad when the city, the place of my father's tombs, lies waste, and its gates have been consumed by fire?"*

Now, friends, Nehemiah's message is a master class in diplomacy. Notice how he avoided mentioning Jerusalem by name. And that omission was intentional because he knew the word "Jerusalem" had negative connotations for a Persian king. The city had been a seedbed for rebellion, so he would not mention it by name. Then he explained his connection to the city where his ancestors were buried: "So, King Artaxerxes, I need to talk to you. Yes, I am brokenhearted because my homeland, my city, the place where my loved ones are buried, is in ruins." Nehemiah helped Artaxerxes understand his connection to the city. He explained the nature of the crisis and how the people of God were in crisis. Cautious about his words but very clear in his intentions, he said what was needed: "Artaxerxes, I know you stopped construction in Israel, but it must resume. The Temple must be rebuilt, and those walls must go back up. It must be done."

Friends, it is easy to call out the sins of the powerless. You parents with small kids know this happens, where your kids play nicely together in another room, and suddenly, you hear voices elevating. And then the play turns into a fight. The next thing you know, one of your young children hauls off and hits the other kid. What do you do? Well, immediately, you insert yourself into the situation without hesitation. You break them up and say, "Listen, in this house, we do not tolerate violence. God calls us to peace. We are going to talk through our differences." You might make them apologize to one another, but you have no problem when your little kids are fighting to have moral clarity and confront it.

However, the situation is different when you are in a weak position and the one you need to confront is a boss, commanding officer, governor, president, or person from whom you want acceptance. These cases are difficult because they set us up for loss. If you confront your boss, you might lose your job. If you confront your commanding officer, you might get a dishonorable discharge. Confronting your government might mean fines or imprisonment. This situation is why Michael Josephson writes, "Being honest at the risk of disapproval, lost income or a maimed career; being accountable when owning up to a mistake can get us in trouble, making tough decisions and demands with our kids at the cost of their affection, being fair when we have the power to be otherwise, and following the rules while others get away with whatever they can—these things take moral courage, the inner strength to do what's right even when it costs more than we want to pay."

But friends, that is what it takes to be a courageous, moral leader. People with moral courage do not do the right thing only when it is easy. They do it when it is difficult, when it could mean loss. Reformers speak up with wisdom and clarity, even if it is dangerous. Then, they pursue a course to rectify the wrong. Look at Verse 4: *Then the king said to me, "What would you request?"* Artaxerxes said, "Nehemiah, you have told me why your heart is breaking. But what do you want done about it?" Then, at the end of Verse 4, we read, *So I prayed to the God of heaven.* Again, we see Nehemiah's humanity. He prayed for four months, but at last the moment came, and he wanted it to go just right. He was frightened and unsure what to say or how the King would respond.

So he quickly delivered this brief prayer: "God, please let me say the right thing, and please let the King be receptive to it." But then, in Nehemiah 2:5-8, he offered his well-considered plan when he told the King in Verse 5, *If it is good for the king, and if your servant is good before you, send me to Judah, to the city of my fathers' tombs, that I may rebuild it.* So, he had a plan he had been thinking about for a long time. He said, "Artaxerxes, let us rebuild the holy land, the Temple, the city, and the walls. King, I volunteer to lead the project. Let me return, and I will organize the rebuilding effort myself." His plan included additional details, as we read in Verse 7: *And I said to the king, "If it is good for the king, let letters be given me to the governors of the provinces beyond the River, that they may allow me to pass through until I come to Judah."*

A 750-mile journey separated Nehemiah's place from Jerusalem, so many people along the way were curious about why this Israelite was passing through Persia and heading back to the holy land. So Nehemiah said, "King, I will need a letter from you so that everybody who stops me along the way knows I have your permission to go." He offered additional details about his plan in Verse 8: *And [send] a letter to Asaph the keeper of the king's forest, that he may give me timber to make beams for the gates of the fortress which is by the house of God, for the wall of the city and for the house to which I will go.* He explained: "So, King, I have a plan. There are forests around the holy land. [We know Lebanon was famous for its forests and quality wood.] So give me another letter permitting me to harvest some of the wood from your forest, and we will use that wood to build the temple and the gates. We also will build a house for me because I will be there for a while."

How did the King reply? We read about it in Verse 6: *Then the king said to me, the queen sitting beside him, "How long will your journey be, and when will you return?"* In the same verse, Nehemiah also writes, *So it was good to the king to send me, and I gave him a set time.* It was the best possible response. He prayed and was scared, but he went forward anyway. He prayed during the conversation and laid out the problem and then a solution. He offered to finish the work himself, and the King said yes to everything: "Yes, you can go. You can have my timber. You can rebuild." Everything went exactly right.

V. Giving God the glory every step of the way. Now let us look at how Nehemiah ended his story in Verse 8: *And the king granted them to me because the good hand of my God was on me.* Here, we see the last quality of godly reformers with moral courage: They give the glory to God every step of the way. You know, friends, God was the hero of this story. It was not Nehemiah, King Artaxerxes, or anybody else. The hero was God. He did the work. He providentially allowed his people to return to the Holy Land by working in King Cyrus' heart, the king who allowed them to start going back into Israel. He worked in Artaxerxes' heart to grant permission for the rebuilding. God was the true hero in this story. He did a new work among his people, revived them, and brought about a complete national reformation.

VI. Concluding thoughts. Today's passage profiles moral courage, which may be a godly reformer's most fundamental character quality—the ability to stand up for what is right and not to back down, even in the face of danger. Nehemiah, John Calvin, and every person God has used from the beginning until now to bring good to his people have modeled this quality. And in all of these examples, friends, whether it is Nehemiah or Calvin, what we have are only faint reflections of the moral courage of Jesus Christ, the one who came, lived, died, and rose again for us, the one who was silent in the face of his persecutors, the one who experienced death and hell for our sakes. He was the ultimate display of courage, and we are called to be like him.

VII. Suggestions for developing moral courage. How do we develop moral courage on our own? We can begin by solidifying our core convictions. We need to decide from the Scriptures what the hills worth dying on are and what truths, virtues, institutions, and people are so important that they transcend our safety and lives. We must develop our core, cement it down as the foundation of our lives, and say, "I am willing to fight for these principles." We must develop that core and resolve to stand for convictions no matter what. Let us pray for the grace to keep that resolution. We also need to draw strength from the heroes of the past, such as Nehemiah, Luther, Calvin, and especially Jesus Christ.

Finally, we need to learn how to be faithful in the small things. Every day, we can take a moral stand, whether in our households, with our young kids, in the workplace, or wherever we are. Let us learn to be courageous in the small things and build up our spiritual muscles, so they will be ready when needed for the big challenges. Friends, the big things will come our way. May we always get into the habit of giving God the credit for every moral success, for the victory will be his in the end.

CHAPTER FOUR

REBUILDING OUR MISSIONAL FOCUS

GODLY REFORMERS ARE MISSIONAL LEADERS.

I. Introduction to sermon on Nehemiah 2:9-20. My friends, God does not just call us to be leaders in this world. He calls us to be missional leaders who understand that there is a mission to complete and have confidence about who we are in Christ, what we stand for, the task that lies before us, and how to accomplish that task. We need leaders who are determined to see the task through, even when there is opposition. This is the need of the hour for mission-driven spiritual leaders. If you need a compelling example of this kind of leadership, look no further than Nehemiah.

If you are unfamiliar with Nehemiah's story, he was an Israelite living in Persia many centuries ago, but he was also a very godly man with a heart for God's people. It broke his heart when he learned that the Israelites in the Holy Land were in a beleaguered state. To know that the city of Jerusalem was still lying in ruins and that God's people were spiritually discouraged was unbearable for Nehemiah. For months, he mourned, fasted, prayed, brainstormed, and thought that maybe God could use him to help spark a national rebuilding and revival.

Finally, the Lord put it into his heart to approach King Artaxerxes of Persia and ask him for permission to return to Jerusalem and lead the effort in a national revival. God was with Nehemiah, and he gave him the courage. He also worked in King Artaxerxes' heart. Nehemiah spoke to the King, who was sympathetic to the request and permitted Nehemiah to return. The King even gave Nehemiah a series of letters to take with him, including one letter explaining a change in Persia's policy. Artaxerxes had previously opposed rebuilding the Holy Land, but now he was permitting it. Another letter permitted Nehemiah to harvest timber from the King's forest so the Israelites could rebuild the walls and gates of Jerusalem. This is where we were in the story when we left off last week.

II. Missional leaders set out with purpose. Nehemiah received approval to leave Susa, where he was living at the time, to go on a 750-mile journey to Jerusalem and finish a building project in the Israeli capital city. Now, we move to Nehemiah 2:9, where Nehemiah had completed his journey. There is no record of the journey itself; we simply find him in the Holy Land. Let us begin with Verse 9, where Nehemiah writes, *Then I came to the governors of the province beyond the River.* So he made a long journey, crossed the Euphrates, and entered the Holy Land. There, he met with provincial governors beyond the River.

He gave those leaders the King's letters that permitted him to harvest the King's timber. Nehemiah had more than just the King's letters, however. The end of Verse 9 says, *Now the King had sent with me commanders of the military force and horsemen.* Not only did he have the King's letters, but he also had the King's military with him, including infantry and cavalry, which was undoubtedly King Artaxerxes's idea. They showed Artaxerxes's love for his cupbearer, Nehemiah, that he would ensure safe passage to Jerusalem by giving him this military entourage. It guaranteed him safe passage and also helped clarify King Artaxerxes' new policy that, yes, indeed, they could rebuild Jerusalem. More importantly, it meant Nehemiah entered the Holy Land in style, which was cool.

But now we come to Verse 10. No sooner did Nehemiah land in the Holy Land than he began to experience opposition from two adversaries: *Sanballat the Horonite* and *Tobiah the Ammonite official*. A document discovered by archaeologists identifies Sanballat as the governor of Samaria, a province north of Judea, so this guy was a big deal. We also have documents dated to this time period with his name on them, so we know that Tobiah was the governor of Ammon, a province northeast of Jerusalem. Nehemiah had come a long way, about 750 miles, to get from Susa to Jerusalem. The journey had been arduous, but he was on a mission, so he was willing to endure the trials of a long trip. Now he had arrived, and immediately, he had powerful adversaries to contend with.

Verse 10 explains why Nehemiah's presence upset these two men: *It was a great evil to them that someone had come to seek the good of the sons of Israel.* Nehemiah had been willing to make this journey and face all the adversities because he was a man on a mission who wanted to see Israel rise from the ruins, to see that nation become a light to the Gentiles again, and to see the people in Israel flourishing once more. He wanted God to be glorified through this chosen nation, which drove everything. Nehemiah believed that God had put this mission into his heart, so he faced these opponents who did not want what he wanted. Sanballot and Tobiah led provinces near Judea and thus were perfectly happy for Jerusalem to remain in ashes and for the Jewish capital city to remain without walls. A spiritually discouraged people strengthens the hands of the enemies around them.

How would Nehemiah handle these powerful adversaries? We find out at the beginning of Verse 11, where Nehemiah writes, *So I came to Jerusalem.* I love these words because they show that nothing will deter this man from his task, not even the governors of rival provinces. Nothing would stop him after these hundreds of miles of travel. Do you think two politicians would stop him? No way. He kept on going. You see, friends, nothing will shake your resolve when you are convinced of your divine mandate. Jerusalem was a long way from Susa, but that distance did not stop Nehemiah. As he got closer to the city, rival provinces began to make threatening postures, but those threats would not stop him. Nothing was going to deter him.

Friends, true leadership requires this kind of resolve. Where does its resolve come from? It begins with a clear sense of mission. Knowing who you are in Christ and what God would have you do is all you need to face any difficulty. It helped Nehemiah continue with his journey. A sense of purpose always drives missional leaders. They continue on with purpose.

III. Missional leaders make honest assessments about the current state of affairs. Now, we come to Nehemiah 2:11-15, which says, *So I came to Jerusalem and was there three days.* What was Nehemiah doing for those three days? The text does not say, but we can surmise that he rested for much of it after his long journey. He needed to rest, and you should understand that there is nothing ungodly about resting occasionally. Sometimes, a nap is the godliest thing you can do. In Mark 6:31, Jesus tells his disciples, *"Come away by* *yourselves to a desolate place and rest a while. (For there were many people coming and going, and they did not even have time to eat.)*

There is no conflict between being a mission-driven leader and a leader who understands your physical limitations. You will not do yourself or anybody else any good if you go nonstop without a break. You will burn out, not finish your task, and reap no benefits from your labors. It is good for us to realize that we are not God, that our bodies get tired, and that sometimes we need to pause and recuperate, which Nehemiah did. He took three days to rest, but I also believe he may have been doing something else during these three days: meeting with various people in Jerusalem, including priests, nobles, officials, and city residents. He started to form relationships with key people because he would need them to carry out his work.

Then we come to Verse 12. After his three-day rest and possible meet-and-greet period, Nehemiah writes, *And I arose in the night, I and a few men with me. I did not tell anyone what my God was putting into my heart to do for Jerusalem; and there was no animal with me except the animal on which I was riding.* So Nehemiah came into Jerusalem with these letters from King Artaxerxes, which a few people had seen. The governors of rival provinces knew what Nehemiah was doing, but the masses in Israel were unaware of his plans, which included bringing about a national reformation, rebuilding Jerusalem, and helping God's people flourish again.

Nehemiah chose to keep them in the dark for a while because it would do no good for him to rush into Jerusalem and say, "Hey everybody, I am here to rebuild your nation. Let us go do it." They would reply, "Who is this guy? We do not know you. You do not know us. You do not know what life is like here. We cannot do what you say." So you see, Nehemiah needed to take some time to get to know the people first, build some rapport with them and then take a journey around Jerusalem to see its state with his own eyes. He needed to see how bad the condition of the city was so that afterward, he could go to the people and say, "Look, I have seen with my own eyes what we are up against. I know what this city has gone through. I plan to get us from this point to where we need to be." Leaders operate this way.

So Nehemiah took a night journey while everyone else was asleep—just him, his donkey, and perhaps a few guides. They began their trip around the city walls. Verse 13 details this journey: *So I went out at night by the Valley Gate.* This gate was on the western side of the city. Of course, there was no standing gate, so he walked through its rubble. Then he made a sharp left turn and went down to the Dragon Spring, south along Jerusalem's western side. Dragon Spring used to be a beautiful place, with the Pool of Siloam and a lovely garden. Of course, it was a pile of debris, but he was making his way around the city's perimeter. Nehemiah went next to the Dung Gate from the Dragon Gate, which was located at the city's southern tip. As its name suggests, this gate was where the residents of Jerusalem would dump all of their refuse. Outside that gate was the vast Valley of Hinnom, Jerusalem's landfill.

So Nehemiah made his circuit around the city, going south, reaching the bottom tip, and climbing upward in a large horseshoe formation. In Verse 13, he writes that he was *inspecting the walls of Jerusalem which were broken down and its gates which were consumed by fire*. So, as he made this ring around the city, he paid close attention to all the work that must be done. In Verse 14, he writes, *Then I passed on to the Spring Gate* on the city's eastern edge. Now, he was heading further north. At the end of Verse 14, Nehemiah writes, *But there was no place for my animal to pass*. At this point in the circuit, he encountered a pile of debris that was so massive and unstable that his donkey could not traverse it. So, Nehemiah dismounted and continued on foot.

Interestingly, in 1961, an archaeologist named Kathleen Kenyon unearthed a massive pile of rubble at this exact spot. She concluded that it was left behind by King Nebuchadnezzar's conquest of Jerusalem in 586 BC. This debris was undoubtedly the same pile Nehemiah had encountered. So the city had been in ruins for over a hundred years, and Nebuchadnezzar had destroyed the city wall so his army could march through. However, the ruins remained, and Nehemiah and his animals could not pass together, so he dismounted and proceeded on foot in a more circuitous route around the rubble.

In Verse 15, Nehemiah writes, *So I went up at night by the ravine and inspected the wall*. At this point, he was outside that debris field, hugging the valley's edge that wrapped around the city's east side, and continued to inspect everything he could. At the end of Verse 15, he writes, *Then I turned and entered the Valley Gate and turned around*. So he doubled back, retraced his steps, and reentered the city at the point where he departed. Nehemiah's now-completed tour gave him a clear view of Jerusalem's condition.

Friends, here we see another important leadership principle: You need to know your starting point before moving people toward your goal. It requires a careful assessment of the present state of affairs and looking at the task at hand from an objective viewpoint. Someone explained this to me years ago: The difference between a dreamer and a leader is that a dreamer can imagine a better future for people, but a leader knows all the steps required to get from where they are now to that better state. Nehemiah is clearly a leader with a powerful sense of mission.

IV. Missional leaders rally the faithful. Nehemiah carefully inspected Jerusalem to know exactly where the rebuilding stood because he knew where he wanted to be. At this point, he could determine the steps to get from here to there. And now that he had completed all this challenging work, he was ready to rally the faithful. We see this in Verse 17, where Nehemiah started with the negative and then turned to the positive. But let us go back to what he writes in Verse 16: *Now the officials did not know where I had gone or what I was doing; nor had I as yet told the Jews, the priests, the nobles, the officials, or the rest who were doing the work.* In Verse 17, he was ready to start getting some buy-in for this project, so he began with the negative: *Then I said to them, "You see the calamity we are in, that Jerusalem lies waste and its gates burned by fire."*

So Nehemiah, having made the journey, pressed through the adversaries and inspected matters for himself, spoke to the masses in Jerusalem, and was honest with them. A leader must always be honest with the people. And he said to the residents of Jerusalem, "I am not going to sugarcoat this. You and I both see it. We are in trouble. Things are not good here right now." He could not even circle the entire city because the debris fields were so extensive. The city was clearly in physical trouble. It was vulnerable to foreign invasions, it had no walls for protection, and the people were in psychological trouble, feeling weak, defeated, and spiritually troubled. After all, God had set up this nation as a light to the Gentiles, but what Gentile could take it seriously? The Gentile nations had cities with walls. Israel, God's chosen nation, was a pile of ashes.

This entire situation was a spiritual crisis, too, and they all felt it. But notice something very important here in Nehemiah's words: the pronouns he used. He told the residents of Jerusalem, "You see the trouble that 'we' are in. Nehemiah was born and raised in Persia and served in Susa, the King's winter resort. But notice how he identified himself with God's people in Israel here. He was an Israelite, and he identified with the Israelites. Here is another essential quality in leadership. It will not do for a man to say, "Look, you guys, you are really in trouble here. But do not worry. I am here to save you from it." No, there must not be a barrier between the leader and his people. There must be a sense that everyone is in this together, and that is what Nehemiah did. He said, "We are in this mess. We are living in this heap of ash. But together, we can get out of it. Together, we can be all God would have us be again."

In the second part of Verse 17, Nehemiah writes, *Come, let us rebuild the wall of Jerusalem*. He said, "Yes, we are in trouble, but we can fix it. We can rebuild the walls, and look what will happen if we do: *We will no longer be a reproach*. Until now, God's people have been an object of ridicule from all the nations surrounding them: "Look at these people. They claim to be God's chosen people. We are in the Holy Land. Look at it. It is in ruins. Who can take these people seriously?" Nehemiah said, "I see we are in bad shape. But together, if we catch a vision of what God would have us to be again, and if together, we pick up our shovels and get to work, we can be all that God would have us to be. We can rebuild this city. We do not have to live among the ruins any longer. We can be a shining city on a hill. We can be a place where people are once again drawn to the God of Heaven. It can all happen. We can do it together." The best leaders are inspirational. They help their people see the possibilities and then see how, if they work together, they will achieve them.

In Verse 18, Nehemiah explains to the people why this goal is not just some pipe dream. They had a genuine basis for believing that a national reformation could occur. He writes, *And I told them how the hand of my God has been good to me and also about the King's words which he had said to me*. He essentially said, "Listen, you residents of Jerusalem. We live among the ruins, but it does not have to be that way. We can rebuild this place and make it all it ought to be. And here is how I know it. Months and months ago, when I heard the news about the sorry state of Jerusalem, I began to pray, fast, brainstorm, and beg God to do something new among his people. And then I asked God to use me to do it."

Then Nehemiah explained to the people that God answered his prayers: "God gave me the courage to confront the most powerful man in the world, King Artaxerxes, and to tell Artaxerxes of my desire, knowing that he [the Persian King] was the one who had ordered the stop to the construction of Jerusalem. But I went to him, looked him in the eye, and told him that God had put it into my heart to rebuild." Nehemiah then explained how God had answered that request: "Artaxerxes said yes to me, that I could go. He presented me with letters that gave me access to construction materials so we could build and letters announcing the change in policy so that nobody could stop us. And the King also gave me a contingent of soldiers to guarantee safe passage." But he told the Israelites even more than that: "God has been with me every step of the way. I know that God is with us now. We can rebuild the walls. God will do it for us. He will work with us. God wants to make a name for himself in our nation again. It can be done."

Nehemiah gave the people a vision of what could be done and explained how the work could be done, that they had reason for confidence in the plan because they had God with them. So, friends, we see here that Nehemiah set out with a purpose. He gave his plan an honest assessment and rallied the faithful. Now, it was time to get to work. What was the response of the residents of Jerusalem? Here is my favorite sentence from the book, where they reply to Nehemiah in Verse 18: *Let us arise and build. So they strengthened their hands for the good work.* They fully bought into what Nehemiah was saying. They responded by saying, "Yes, Nehemiah. Let us do it. Let us rise up, rebuild from these ashes, and build ourselves a city. Let us build ourselves a nation, revive the people of God, and do something great together." So they began the work.

V. Missional leaders are undeterred by the naysayers. And so we come to Verse 19, where Nehemiah writes about more trouble: *But Sanballat the Horonite and Tobiah the Ammonite official and Geshem the Arab heard it.* In other words, they heard that the Israelites had rallied to do a great thing. As soon as they became aware of it, *They mocked us and despised us and said, "What is this thing you are doing? Are you rebelling against the King?"* We had already met Sanballat and Tobiah, but who was this new character, Geshem the Arab? He was the most powerful adversary of them all. Years ago, archaeologists unearthed a silver vessel donated to an Arabian goddess. On it was the name Geshem, King of Kedar. This vessel, combined with other documents that archeologists have uncovered, revealed that Geshem the Arab was a ruler of an entire league of Arab tribes south of Judea.

So now Nehemiah was surrounded by adversaries: Sanballat and Tobiah to the north and northeast, and Geshem the Arab with his entire league of tribes to the south, southeast, and southwest of Israel. Opponents surrounded Jerusalem, and they employed a threefold strategy to stop Nehemiah. First, they used ridicule: *They mocked us.* This tactic is a frequent tool used by the enemies of God. They try to make God's people appear dumb or foolish, make them feel small and vulnerable, and convince them that nobody takes them seriously, so they should not take themselves too seriously either. The enemies of God are very good at using ridicule. I once read a statement that the Church of Jesus Christ can endure persecution. We can endure imprisonment and martyrdom, but can we endure being the target of other people's jokes? Can we endure social scorn? That is a real test.

These three powerful men employed ridicule to stop God's people, but they also used contempt. Nehemiah writes, *And [they] despised us.* In doing so, they poured out their angry vitriol on them. God's people also face the vitriol of the masses, do they not? But friends, when this happens, remember our Lord's words in Matthew 5:11-12, when he says, *"Blessed are you when people insult you and persecute you, and falsely say all kinds of evil against you because of Me. Rejoice and be glad, for your reward in heaven is great; for in the same way they persecuted the prophets who were before you."* We also see they used threats of harm, another common tool used against God's people. Notice what they said to Nehemiah: *What is this thing you are doing? Are you rebelling against the King?* We can read between the lines here. They said, "Nehemiah, it would be a shame if word got back to Artaxerxes that you were trying to foment a new rebellion here. You would not want the King to hear that, would you?" It was the threat of arrest, imprisonment, torture, and maybe death: "You are not rebelling against the King, are you?"

Friends, sometimes God's enemies will make threats because they do not know something that God's people do know, which is found in 2 Corinthians 12:10, where Paul writes, *Therefore I am well content with weaknesses, with insults, with distresses, with persecutions and hardships, for the sake of Christ, for when I am weak, then I am strong.* The enemies of God's people will always use these strategies. From Nehemiah's day to ours, it has always been this way and will always be this way. They will laugh at you and ridicule you. They will write skits about you for *Saturday Night Live* and make you feel as marginalized as possible. They will let you know you are hated and despised and threaten you. They will tell you, "Keep up what you are doing, and we will arrest you. We will take away your property and separate you from your loved ones. We will send you to the stake." That is what they will do. But they do not know that we are strong when we, as God's people, are weak. We rejoice in mistreatments, not because we enjoy being mistreated, but because we know how God can use people who endure it. We know the Gospel spreads when God's people are most mistreated. As one Church father, Tertullian, said, "The blood of the martyrs is the seed of the church."

So Nehemiah replied to his adversaries with these strong words in Verse 20: *So I responded to them with a word and said to them, "The God of heaven will give us success; therefore we His slaves will arise and build, but you have no portion, right, or remembrance in Jerusalem."* He said, "We do not fear you, your threats, or your kings. We have a divine mandate for this project, and we will succeed. We are working under the authority of the King of Heaven, and our King is way bigger than yours. We are not afraid of that. As far as ridicule is concerned, you will not deter us. We will pick up our tools and build, and this city will return to life. When we are finished, and Jerusalem's walls are high and strong, and God's people are worshiping in their temple again--when that day comes, and God is once again prospering us--all of you people will be locked outside. You will have no part in this." Friends, this is what it looks like to be a mission-driven leader.

VI. Final applications and conclusion. Though we are not in Israel, and today is not the 5th century BC, we can learn much from Nehemiah's story, beginning with the fact that we have a divine mandate of our own. It is called the Great Commission and comes directly from Jesus in Matthew 28:18-20, where he says, *All authority has been given to Me in heaven and on earth. Go therefore and make disciples of all the nations, baptizing them in the name of the Father and the Son and the Holy Spirit, teaching them to keep all that I commanded you.* There is our mandate, friends. We are to go, open our mouths, speak, and share the words of gospel life, and, as people come to saving faith in Christ, baptize them and teach them everything Christ taught.

Our task is to build the Church of Jesus Christ under his headship and by his grace. God has told us how to carry out this task. He tells us in his Word how the work is to be fulfilled and what to expect. There will be ridicule, vitriol, and threats. For some, there will be actual persecution, which is why the Church in America is not faring so well today. It is why we are not bold in our speech and why we are modifying long-held doctrines of the faith in America and watering down the demands of discipleship: Our sense of mission is clouded by fear. We are overcome with the desire to please nonbelievers rather than to win them to Christ. The Church is not faring well today.

In this hour, we need to rebuild our resolve, become missional leaders, and become a people who do not cower in the face of ridicule, contempt, and threats. We need to be bold and trust that if God has given us work to do, he will grant us success. We may not know the future of our singular local Church, but we know he has promised his global Church's success. We have a part in building that here. Friends, let us learn to be missional leaders. Let us be the kind of leaders that God needs us to be, and may God grant us success here in our city and around the world, just as he gave success to Nehemiah and those who followed him.

CHAPTER FIVE

REBUILDING OUR SYNERGY

IF WE WOULD BE USED OF GOD TO ACHIEVE SOMETHING GREAT, THEN WE MUST LEARN TO WORK TOGETHER IN PERFECT SYNERGY.

I. Introduction to sermon on Nehemiah 3:1-32. We have been in a series on the Book of Nehemiah for about a month and have a few months to go. If you are not sure who Nehemiah was, he was an Israelite who lived in Persia about 2,500 years ago and worked in King Artaxerxes' court. He was also a very godly man, and when he learned about the sorry state of God's people in Israel, it broke his heart. Nehemiah began fasting, praying, brainstorming, and thinking about how God might use him to revitalize his people in Israel. Finally, with God's help, he developed a plan, took it to King Artaxerxes, and asked him for permission to leave Persia, return to Israel, and help God's people start rebuilding their nation.

Nehemiah understood that this work must begin in Jerusalem, the capital city, by rebuilding the city's walls. Artaxerxes granted permission, and Nehemiah traveled to Jerusalem on a 750-mile journey from Susa, where he was located. We have been following Nehemiah's story as he wrestled with what to do, developed his plans, and begun to implement them. We are studying this book together, hoping to learn some leadership principles to help us achieve something great in our lives. Friends, we want to be used by God to make disciples of the Lord Jesus Christ, build his Church, and revitalize struggling sister churches. If God wills, he will use us to transform the world with the Gospel of Christ.

We want to be used by God to do great things. So, we are studying this book and learning how God used Nehemiah to transform a nation. We hope that God will use this book to help us advance his cause today, and we have already learned a lot from it. For example, if we are to be used by God to achieve great things, we must become a people of prayer because reformation and revival are works of God. If we witness these events in our day, God must take the initiative, so we must pray to God and plead with him to do a spiritual work that we can then participate in.

We have learned that we must be people of moral courage, which means we must be willing to say what needs to be said and do what needs to be done—even at the risk of danger—because God is pleased to use courageous people. We have also learned that we must become mission-driven people and clearly understand who we are in Christ, what he would have us to do, and how he would have us achieve the mission. Then, we must pursue it with all of our hearts.

We are in Nehemiah 3 today and will learn another lesson: If we are to be used by God to achieve something great, we must also learn to work together in perfect synergy. Now, what do I mean by synergy? Please allow me to illustrate. Picture a beautiful golden timepiece in your mind. As you look at the face of that timepiece, understand that it has only one purpose: to give you the correct time of day. However, we also know that accomplishing this single purpose requires many different parts that all work in harmony. If you turn that timepiece around and remove the backing, you will find a bewildering array of parts: hairspring, balance wheel, barrel, bridge, caliber, escapement, and gasket. You will find jewels and a rotor, repeater, shock absorber, battery, computer chip, and many other pieces. But you also will notice how all these parts perfectly interlock and work together to give you the time of day. Well, friends, that is synergy. It has many different parts working together to achieve a singular mission.

In today's text, we find an example of synergy on a grand scale as Nehemiah rallies an entire city to rebuild Jerusalem's walls. However, please note the following before we enter the text. My usual practice is to work phrase by phrase and line by line from the beginning to the end of a passage, offering you an exposition of it in its entirety. But this morning's text is unusual because it does not have a narrative flowing through the chapter. Instead, God's Word lists names, work assignments, and locations where the work was done. It does not lend itself well to a verse-by-verse exposition, so I have gleaned six enduring lessons about building synergy from the chapter and will present them to you by drawing on verses from all over the chapter to make each lesson memorable. The first lesson about synergy is that if we work together as the people of God, we must take personal ownership of the work.

II. Synergy requires everyone to take personal ownership of the work. One of the most beautiful aspects of today's text is how Nehemiah rallied the entire city of Jerusalem behind a single mission: rebuilding the city walls. Virtually every citizen took personal ownership of the work, so Nehemiah achieved nearly 100% buy-in. We also see that the priests were invested in this work. Look at Verse 1 with me: *Then Eliashib the high priest arose with his brothers the priests and built the Sheep Gate; they set it apart as holy and made its doors stand.* Jerusalem's high priest was undoubtedly the city's most prestigious man. His regular work was to lead God's people in worship at the Temple. All of the jobs of his subordinate priests facilitated worship, too. A priest would not ordinarily get involved in a construction project, but Nehemiah sought investment from everyone, so even the high priest and all his subordinates bought into the job and were ready to get to work.

Notice how the tradesmen got to work in Verse 8: *Uziel the son of Harhaiah of the goldsmiths* bought into the project. We also read about other tradesmen getting involved: *Hananiah, one of the perfumers* in Verse 8, *Malchijah* in Verse 31, and other *goldsmiths and the merchants* in Verse 32. So, the high priest and his subordinate priests were invested in this work. And we also see goldsmiths, perfumers, and merchants—all of the tradesmen of Jerusalem—invested in it and prepared to set aside their regular labor for rebuilding the walls.

We even see government officials involved. Imagine government bureaucrats eager to roll up their sleeves and get their hands dirty on a construction project. Nehemiah writes in Verse 9, *Next to them Rephaiah, the son of Hur, the official of half the district of Jerusalem, made repairs.* In Verse 12, *Shallum the son of Hallohesh* was involved. In Verse 14, *Malchijah the son of Rechab, the official of the district of Beth-haccherem, repaired the Dung Gate.* In Verse 15, *Shallum the son of Col-hozeh, the official of the district of Mizpah, repaired the Spring Gate.* And in Verse 16, "*After him Nehemiah the son of Azbuk [a different man named Nehemiah], official of half the district of Beth-zur, made repairs as far as a point opposite the tombs of David.* Here, we see an excellent array of important government officials, including rulers of Jerusalem districts and other surrounding towns and villages, who bought into Nehemiah's vision of rebuilding Jerusalem and readied themselves to invest in the work.

In Verse 17, we also see that the Levites, who served in the Temple as musicians, guards, and gatekeepers, got involved with full buy-in. The temple servants, the Levites' assistants, got involved, which Nehemiah writes in Verse 26. Nehemiah also writes in Verse 22 that all men in the surrounding area got invested in the work. And then, in Verse 12, even women and children got involved. Note this beautiful passage in Verse 12: *Next to him Shallum the son of Hallohesh, the official of half the district of Jerusalem, made repairs, he and his daughters.* A major politician was so invested in the project that he ensured his whole family got involved. He brought his little girls, who helped him rebuild the walls. Nehemiah 3 clearly shows that virtually every person in Jerusalem, from the greatest to the least, was invested in Nehemiah's vision. They all took ownership of this rebuilding project, and everyone desired to do their part. Nobody said, "Look, this is Nehemiah's vision; let him do the job." They said, "It is our vision and mission; let us rebuild the walls."

My friends, can we apply this to our own setting now? We are all members of the body of Christ as fellow believers in this age. Understand that God has given a mission to his body, which is most clearly articulated in Matthew 28:19-20 where Jesus states, "*Go therefore and make disciples of all the nations, baptizing them in the name of the Father and the Son and the Holy Spirit, teaching them to keep all that I commanded you.*" That is the mission of the Church today. Christ has also ordained an institution to carry it out: the local Church, a microcosm of Christ's universal body, a local manifestation of his universal Church. Christ has entrusted to the local Church the work of evangelizing, baptizing, and teaching all that Christ taught. This is our mission. The only way we will succeed in this mission as a church is if every last one of us buys into our Lord's commission. If we also make his great commission our own personal missions, there must be 100% buy-in. Every member of this church must fully commit to the task that our Lord has given us.

Friends, as we consider this task, we would do well to ask ourselves these questions: What is my life all about? What is the driving passion in my life? It would be good for us all to ask ourselves why I came to this church. What brought me here? What keeps me here? Am I driven by the mission our Lord has given me, or do other pursuits drive my life? Have I bought into the idea that I am here on this earth and at this church to make disciples? Friends, gospel ministry requires synergy, and synergy begins when each of us takes personal ownership of the mission. Will you take ownership of it yourself? Now let us explore another lesson about synergy: Everyone must be actively involved in the work.

III. Synergy requires everyone to be actively involved in the work. After Nehemiah achieved 100% buy-in with everyone fully invested in the project, the citizens of Jerusalem rolled up their sleeves and did their assigned work. Here is another beautiful feature of today's text: These city residents paid more than lip service to the mission. Virtually everyone was actively rebuilding the walls. For example, Verse 1 states that the high priest of Jerusalem and the priests under him built the Sheep Gate with their own hands. Verse 2 states that *Next to him the men of Jericho built, and next to them Zaccur the son of Imri built.* The building activities, described from Verse 4 through the entire chapter, list the men, women, and children who got their hands dirty and who did the work. Every household and laborer in Jerusalem was given an assignment, and the entire city worked side by side to rebuild the city wall. They were like an incredible human chain encircling the whole city, raising up the walls together.

Another interesting feature is how Nehemiah ensured everyone on the project was assigned a part of the wall that would be most meaningful to them. In Verses 10, 17, 23, 24, and 28-30, it is evident that Nehemiah did not randomly assign people their jobs. He looked at the volunteers before him, along with a map of Jerusalem, and figured out where each of his volunteers lived in relation to the city's wall. Then, Nehemiah assigned each worker and each household to repair that portion of the wall nearest his own house. Or, he assigned government officials a section of the wall closest to the district they governed. Nehemiah assigned these work projects intentionally. He wanted each person to be given a place on the wall that would be most meaningful to them. He knew that assigning a man to work across from his own house would highly motivate him to do a good job because every day, he would look out the window of his home at the section of the wall he built. He wanted each person to look at the wall and say, "Look at the good job I did. Look at this, kids. Look what we accomplished." Everyone did an excellent job because it was near their houses.

Now, friends, here at our church, we have many different kinds of people, just like they had in Jerusalem. We have men and women, young and old, people with varying experiences of life, educational backgrounds, and ethnicities. Yet, we are all here together by God's providence to form a single local church. God would have us working together to advance the biblical mission. If I can put it this way, he wants each one of us to find a place on the wall to build in this great work. You may have been coming to worship here for a while but have been hesitant to join. Or you may have joined already but have yet to find a place of service. Let me encourage you this morning. If membership is the step you must take, do not let your fears hold you back. Take that step and request membership. For both our new members and those who have been here a while but have not gotten involved, talk to us, and we will find a place of meaningful service for you. We have a place on the wall for you, a place of significance where your contribution means something. We will find that place for you and get you plugged in.

But even though each of us should have a desirable service that fits our unique talents and abilities, there will always be work to do that is less than glamorous. Each of us must be willing to do that kind of work, which takes us to poor Malchijah in Verse 14. His job was to repair the Dung Gate. I can imagine the lunch whistle going off and all the workers in Jerusalem taking out their lunch pails, sitting on the grass, and forming their social circles. They begin to talk about their various projects. One says, "I am rebuilding the section in front of my home." Another says, "I get to shore up the foundation of the great tower." Still, another family says, "We get to replant the king's garden beside the wall." And I imagine another person saying, "We get to cleanse the water of the Pool of Siloam." They were given incredible building assignments, but when they come to Malchijah, they ask, "What are you working on?" And he has to confess, "I am building the Dung Gate."

Friends, not every job will be glamorous, but every job is necessary and needs to get done. You may be a gifted instrumentalist and believe you should use that gift to serve the church. However, understand that there may be times when you need to vacuum the carpet. Or maybe you love leading Bible studies and are good at it and want the opportunity to lead a Bible study, but you also may need to be placed on the nursery rotation so we do not ask the same ladies in the nursery room every week to miss out on the gathered worship service. Or perhaps you would like to go to the range with the security team guys. You should be able to do that, but there also may be times when you need to run the leaf blower outside. You all get the point.

Everyone should have an area of service that is meaningful to them and harmonizes well with their talents, experiences, and abilities. However, because we are a community here, we must all be ready to help with the less-than-glamorous work. None of it is busy work. All of it is essential. This is what synergy is all about: We all take ownership of the work, and then we all get to work. We find out where we can be most helpful and where we are needed, and then we work together to achieve something great. This is synergy. It requires 100% buy-in and everyone to roll up their sleeves and work. Now, we will learn the third lesson of the text, which involves everyone seeing how their individual parts contribute to the overarching mission.

IV. Synergy requires each of us (as we work) to see how our individual parts contribute to the overarching mission. We must know how our slice of the work contributes to the great whole. We see this in today's text in Verse 3: *Now the sons of Hassenaah built the Fish Gate*, which was at the northern tip of the city. In Verse 14, *Malchijah the son of Rechab, the official of the district of Beth-haccherem, repaired the Dung Gate*, which was on the southern tip of the city. We read in Verse 29 that *Shemaiah the son of Shecaniah, the keeper of the East Gate, made repairs*. And then, in Verse 6, we read that *Joiada the son of Paseah and Meshullam the son of Besodeiah repaired the Old Gate*s on the western side. So we have all points of the compass represented: north, south, west, and east.

Friends, as these work assignments were being handed out, it must have been clear to everyone that Nehemiah aimed to revitalize the city. Every part of the wall would be rebuilt, and each section would be assigned a worker. Every worker would have understood that he contributed to a greater whole. So, an individual might have said, "Look, my job is to shore up the foundation of this tower," or "My job is to repair this six-foot section of wall." However, each person also understood that every task was part of a grand project. They worked side by side with everyone else. The short wall section that one family worked on would contribute to rebuilding the entire wall, which would contribute to rebuilding the entire capital city of Israel and revitalizing the nation. Every small job had a part to play in the grand mission.

As a congregation, it is good for us to keep a view of our overarching mission. We are here to make disciples of the Lord Jesus Christ. It is also good for us to understand how every task we accomplish as a church contributes to that grand mission. We must not allow ourselves to get trapped in ministry silos where we become good at our job but have no idea how we are contributing to anything greater. Every job here must trace a line directly from that job to the disciple-making mission, and we must all see how it is done. For example, how do the nursery workers contribute to the disciple-making ministry of our church? When our nursery workers care for all the newborns, the parents and grandparents can sit in the auditorium free of distraction, which means they get to hear the Scripture readings, participate in the hymns, listen to the prayers, and hear the exposition of Scripture without the constant distraction that a newborn brings. Providing baby care during the service allows us to make disciples here.

Or how does a groundskeeper contribute to the mission of disciple-making? If the groundskeeper makes our property look beautiful, it leaves a good impression on new arrivals. And if we make a good impression on new arrivals, we increase their chances of returning and thus extend our opportunities to evangelize and disciple them. Groundskeeping contributes to discipleship. Or how about maintaining the building? If we allow our building to go to mothballs, we will no longer have a place to meet as a congregation. We would need to break up the congregation into small parts and meet in private homes.

Friends, we cannot function as well apart as we can together as one large church family. Maintaining the building is a disciple-making activity. As one final example, our Sunday school teachers do not just occupy our young children. They teach them the truths of Scripture and make disciples of our kids. Every single one of us here has an individualized job, and every job contributes to the great mission of making disciples for Christ. We must understand this truth so that when somebody asks what you do at church, you can say, "I watch newborns in the nursery so their parents can be discipled in the auditorium," or "I mow the lawn so visitors will have a good impression, and we can minister to them." Understand your job and the great purpose it serves. Friends, we know we work well together when we each have our own work assignment and a good understanding of its role in the greater whole. Now, we look at our fourth point.

V. Synergy requires each of us to do our part with perseverance and skill. No worthwhile project will be finished overnight. Everyone must be in it for the long haul and committed to doing a good job. We see this in Verse 3. Notice the care with which this project was undertaken: *The sons of Hassenaah built the Fish Gate; they laid its beams and made its doors stand with its bolts and bars.* You can hear the careful attention to detail in this verse. We read the same details conveyed in Verse 6. Notice in Verse 10 the repetition of the word "repairs." The Israelites worked hard to restore the walls and gates to their former glory. They cleared away the old debris, gathered new materials, and painstakingly fitted everything together to make a beautiful wall and gates. This same perseverance and skill are repeated throughout this chapter. Verse 11 states that another section was repaired, and Verse 13 states that these men repaired more than a quarter mile of wall. We read about everyone persevering in the work and their painstaking efforts to do a good job.

Friends, do not cut corners in your ministries or approach your job half-heartedly. Do not make commitments that you have no intention of keeping. We must all dedicate ourselves to the work God has assigned us. We also must ensure that our job is done correctly and trust that those around us are doing their jobs correctly. Together, we will build something here that endures, which is the fifth lesson about synergy.

VI. Synergy requires each of us to value the contributions of all the others. So far we have read that the people in Jerusalem bought into the mission, rolled up their sleeves, and did an excellent job at their station. However, we also read about how the people loved the work they saw everybody else doing, another notable feature of today's text. We find Nehemiah was careful to give full credit to every worker for every part he had done. Every verse in this chapter is a statement of public recognition. Let us look at a few striking examples.

In Verse 16, Nehemiah gave the worker's name, job assignment, starting point, and finishing point. He was very careful when recognizing this worker. In Verses 24 and 31, Nehemiah wanted to ensure that every person who invested in this work was mentioned by name, that their work assignments were publicly known, and that their good work was publicly recognized. In a healthy community, no one wants to steal the spotlight. They want to share it with everyone doing quality work and credit the entire group for the mission's success. No one is so prideful as to think one part is more important than another. This is synergy.

Friends, here at our church, we devote one Sunday a year to recognize our volunteers publicly. We call it Worker Appreciation Sunday and announce the volunteers' names, explain their work, and then offer a small gift. However, more recognition is needed. Every week, scores of good deeds are done that nobody sees: behind-the-scenes work of praying and sending cards; giving words of kindness; substitute teaching for an ill teacher; picking up a leaf on the carpet and throwing it away because you want the building to look nice; and mudding drywall and sanding old paint away. A thousand little tasks nobody sees are all worthwhile work, and they deserve public recognition.

Let us try our best to build a culture of recognition here so we do not have to wait for a formal service to arrive. If you see somebody doing a noteworthy service, consider saying, "Thank you, ladies, for working in the kitchen while the rest of us enjoy the food in our fellowship hall," or "Thank you for vacuuming," or "Thank you for cleaning so well this week," or "Thank you for the kind words, the card, and the prayer." Let us promote a culture of recognition. Friends, public recognition advances the mission by communicating to everyone that their work matters. Now, let us address our sixth and final lesson about synergy in the Church.

VII. Synergy requires each of us to believe in the spiritual import of our work. Please look once more at Verse 1: *Then Eliashib the high priest arose with his brothers the priests and built the Sheep Gate.* And look what they did next: *They set it apart as holy and made its doors stand. And they set apart as holy the wall to the Tower of the Hundred and the Tower of Hananel.* So, these priests built and then consecrated two towers. To consecrate something is to dedicate it to God. These priests understood they were not just building a wall or erecting a gate. They were doing spiritual work and building a holy city where the people of God could worship him, a city that would be a light on a hill for all nations to see. They were building a home for God's chosen people while understanding the spiritual significance of what they were doing.

Friends, our church is doing spiritual work, too. Even our current renovation is a spiritual effort. Why did we blacktop the parking lot? Why did we enlarge the nursery? Why are we increasing the seating capacity in our auditorium? We are completing these projects to allow more people to gather and worship here. As a result, they will hear the Gospel in our building, and more families can be accommodated. Putting up drywall and laying carpet are spiritual works. Everything we do here is spiritual work—from wiping tables to washing dishes, running the vacuum cleaner, teaching Sunday school, and leading a prayer meeting. It is all done ultimately for the worship of God.

VIII. Conclusion. Let us quickly summarize what we have learned this morning: If we want God to use us to achieve great things in our day, we must learn to work together in perfect synergy. That means we must all take personal responsibility for the work. There must be 100% buy-in, and we must all roll up our sleeves and get to work. We need to understand how each assignment contributes to the greater mission, which means doing our work with perseverance and skill. It also means we value not only our jobs but every assignment in the church family. Furthermore, it means recognizing one another's contributions and then recognizing the spiritual importance of our actions.

All of these components of synergy create a community of faith that works together to see God's work advance. If we work together in perfect synergy, God will be pleased to expand this ministry and give us another 21 years or perhaps another 121 years. We trust our church will be here and thriving until our Lord comes to take us home. Let us work to that end.

Chapter Six

Rebuilding in the Face of Opposition

If we would be used of God to achieve something great, we must be willing to work in the face of opposition.

I. Introduction to sermon on Nehemiah 4:1-23. About two years ago, Aaron Renn published an article in *First Things* entitled "The Three Worlds of Evangelicalism." This article traced the significant movements of secularization in modern American society, its impact on the American church, and the process's division into three eras. He called the first phase The Positive World, which ran from the turn of the 20th century until 1994. In this world, society retained a mostly positive view of Christianity. Biblical moral norms pervaded society; being a Christian even had certain social benefits.

But then America moved out of the Positive World into what he called The Neutral World, which ran from 1994 to 2014. During this phase, society took a neutral stance toward Christianity, neither privileging nor disfavoring it. Biblical moral norms retained a residual presence in society but certainly lost their dominant presence. One could have been religious or non-religious with no impact on social standing. The final phase, which Renn called The Negative World, started in 2014 and continues today. In this phase of American secularization, being a traditional Christian is detrimental to your social status. Biblical morality is seen as harmful, repressive, and even threatening to the public good. Many people look at the Church as the problem, not as the solution to the problem.

Now, friends, I still believe we live in the freest country on planet Earth. Being a Christian and engaging in gospel ministry here is still easier than anywhere else. Yet, we all must acknowledge that it is becoming more challenging to be a faithful Christian than in times past. The pressures are stronger than they once were. Therefore, we need to learn how to do gospel ministry in the face of opposition in the future. This sobering reality is what makes the book of Nehemiah so important.

Nehemiah was an Israelite who lived in Persia about 2,500 years ago. He was also a godly man with a heart for God and his people, so when he learned that God's people in Israel were in a beleaguered state, it broke his heart. He began to fast, pray, and brainstorm ways that God might use him to help revitalize the nation of Israel. Finally, Nehemiah came up with a plan. He went to his boss, King Artaxerxes, and asked permission to leave Susa and return to Jerusalem to help God's people revitalize their nation. Nehemiah understood that if Israel were to be revitalized, it needed to start with its capital city. If Jerusalem were to be revitalized, it needed to begin with rebuilding its city walls. Nehemiah planned to go to Jerusalem and lead a program to rebuild the walls. God worked in King Artaxerxes's heart to permit Nehemiah to undertake this project.

For over a month, we have been following Nehemiah's story, first as he learned about Israel's plight and then as he prayed, fasted, and wrestled with what he could do to help. We have followed him on this long journey back to Jerusalem and have seen him and the workers begin the project. The Book of Nehemiah has taught us many critical lessons about spiritual leadership. For example, we have learned that to accomplish something great for God, we must be a people of prayer. We have also learned that we must be people of moral courage with a clear sense of our mission and work together in perfect synergy. All of these principles are necessary to accomplish God's work today. As we move on to Nehemiah 4, we will learn how to handle opposition to the work. This chapter teaches us that if we are to be used by God to achieve something great, we must persevere in the face of opposition.

II. As we do the Lord's work, we can expect the world's jeers. The following statement bears repetition: If God would use us to achieve something great, we must learn to persevere in the face of opposition. Let us see this together now, starting with Verse 1: *Now it happened that when*

Sanballat heard that we were rebuilding the wall, he became angry and very vexed and mocked the Jews. He spoke in the presence of his brothers and the wealthy men of Samaria and said, "What are these feeble Jews doing? Are they going to restore it for themselves? Can they offer sacrifices? Can they complete it in a day? Can they bring the stones to life from the dusty rubble, though they are burned?"

As we launch into Nehemiah 4, we see an immediate confrontation with adversaries. Nehemiah and his workers were stationed along the perimeter of Jerusalem's wall, laboring to rebuild it, and now they faced opposition. The ringleader of this opposition was a man called Sanballat, the governor of Samaria, a province to the north of Jerusalem with a population hostile to the Jews. When Sanballat found out that the Jews were making progress in rebuilding Jerusalem's walls, he was enraged. Why? Because he saw a revitalized Judea as a threat to the province of Samaria. He believed that if the Jews rose to power, it would cost him power.

Sanballat determined that he would need to stop the revitalization of Israel at all costs. He began with the following strategy: Use ridicule to demoralize the people of God, thus making them give up the work. We see in the first part of Verse 2 that he tried to make the Israelites feel small, saying, "Who are these feeble Jews? It is such a big project. They are so few in number. They do not really think they can do this thing, do they?" He also tried to make them believe their mission is foolish, asking if they can do this job: "What, are they going to do it in a day? Are they going to gather up all of the rubble around their city and somehow fashion it into walls? Are they going to do this?" Sanballat heaped ridicule on the people of God, hoping it would cause them to be demoralized and give up the project.

Then we notice in Verse 3 that Sanballat was not alone: *Now Tobiah the Ammonite was near him.* You may remember Tobiah as well. He was the governor of Ammon, a province to the northeast of Jerusalem. Tobiah added his ridicule to the mix. In the second part of Verse 3, he said, *Even what they are building—if a fox should jump on it, he would break their stone wall down!* So Sanballat, his brothers, and his army were heaping their ridicule, saying, "You Jews, don't you see how feeble you are, how weak you are? Don't you know that you cannot possibly gather up all these ruins and make a city out of them?" And then Tobiah said these cruel words about their craftsmanship: "Look at this thing you are building. You better not let any critters jump on top of it. They are liable to bring it down." Everyone laughed at God's people as they tried to do their work.

You know, friends, ridicule is an easy tool to use. It requires no intellectual labor, no facts, and no arguments. All it takes is the ability to make another person feel silly. However, it can also be an effective tool because it can produce shame, fear, anger, and other negative emotions in the recipient. It can even prompt people to abandon the good work that God would have them do. You do not need to take my word for this. Have you not seen it for yourself in your own life? How many times did you have an opportunity to share the Gospel with one of your co-workers but chose not to seize the moment because you were afraid they would mock you in return? And maybe you feared they would go to your other co-workers and get a good chuckle out of you. It was your fear of ridicule that kept you silent. Some of you schoolchildren, how many times have you seen one of your classmates getting picked on in school? You knew you should have done something to stand up for them, but you did not because of fear. You thought if you stood up for that kid, everyone would turn on you, and you would start getting picked on. You would be the object of ridicule. So you did not do the right thing because you feared being laughed at.

I wonder how many church leaders have stopped contending for the faith because they feared the social media mob: "If I speak the words of God with clarity and conviction, and people in my town hear about it, I will never stop receiving flak. I will get social media posts against me, negative letters to the editor, and harassing phone calls to my church voicemail." They cannot bear the thought of that scorn, so they compromise on the doctrines of Scripture. I wonder how many people have abandoned Christ altogether because they cannot bear to be on the receiving end of other people's jokes. You see, friends, ridicule is a highly effective tool. Even the best of us are susceptible to it, and that is why Sanballat, Tobiah, and all of their followers heaped ridicule on Nehemiah and all those workers on Jerusalem's walls. They thought their cruel verbal attacks would make God's people drop their tools and go home, giving up their good work.

How can we stand up to the world's ridicule? What must we do when it happens? Let us look at Nehemiah's example: We must pray and then press on. It is as simple as that. When the ridicule comes, you pray and press on. Look at Verses 4 and 5, where we find Nehemiah's prayer: *Hear, O our God, for we are despised! Return their reproach on their own heads and give them up for plunder in a land of captivity. Do not forgive their iniquity and let not their sin be blotted out before You, for they have vexed the builders.* This prayer is so important. Nehemiah and all of God's people have endured all of this mockery heaped upon them. We all know the impact it can have on a person. But

Nehemiah took it to God instead of returning it in kind by heaping scorn on their adversaries or responding with violence. When the world despises and scorns you, do not repay them in kind. Go to God and take it to him in prayer.

Some of you may find the content of Nehemiah's prayer very jarring. However, it does not need to be, because I understand what he was doing here. As far as Nehemiah was concerned, Sanballat, Tobiah, and all of their followers were just as hardened in their unbelief as the Pharaoh, who had enslaved their ancestors generations ago. Remember how Pharaoh hardened his heart against God and enslaved the people of God? He was not going to change, so God brought down his judgments on Pharaoh, which was the only way for the Jewish people to be freed. As Nehemiah looked at Sanballat, Tobiah, and the others, he saw the same story repeating itself. Here was a godless group of men hardened in their unbelief. They would not change.

So, notice what Nehemiah prayed: "God, it is not my place to deal with these people, but I know it is your place. You are God. If they are not to be saved, take them out of the way and hasten your judgments, because they are your enemies and fighting against your people and your cause. This cannot be, God. It cannot be. So, God, take them away so that your name can be glorified, your nation can be rebuilt, and your people can be revitalized." His prayer was God-centered from beginning to end. It was a good prayer, the kind of prayer we can offer God when facing the world's anger. We can pray, "God, you know our situation and plight. People are coming at us from all sides with their vitriol. God, we desire their redemption. But if that is not the case, if they have hardened themselves against you, would you do the next best thing and clear them out of our path so we can do your work without hindrance?" That is the right kind of prayer to offer.

But then notice that after Nehemiah prayed, he pressed on in Verse 6: *So we built the wall.* Is that not a beautiful, concise statement? They were getting all of this vitriol but did not respond in kind. Instead, they took it to God and got right back to work. It was time to build that wall again, which they did. Notice how they started making some real progress in the second part of Verse 6: *And the whole wall was joined together to half its height and the people had a heart to work.* In responding this way, Nehemiah made his opponents look very small. They wanted him to look small, but he made them look trivial by ignoring them, simply taking it to God, and persevering. And the work continued.

My friends, if you are committed to doing God's work, you can be sure that you will be ridiculed. Christian parents, as you raise your children in the nurture of the Lord, you can be sure there will be non-believing family members, neighbors, co-workers, and others who look at what you are trying to accomplish and laugh at your efforts: "Do you think you, in this culture, can raise children to know and love God? Can you do that? What a silly thing." They will look at your priorities as a parent and say, "Oh, what a foolish set of priorities you have." They are going to heap ridicule on you.

And Christian members of this church, as you give yourselves to the work of the Lord through this church, there will be ridicule. Others will say, "What are you doing giving all of your time, effort, and financial resources to this church? Why are you doing that? Why do you wake up early on Sunday morning, dress in your best clothes, and attend church? Why not just sleep in? You never get to sleep in. Why do you live like this?" There will be teasing, scorn, and mocking. It will come, and, friends, when it does come, you know what to do: Take it all to God in prayer. Cast that burden on him because He cares for you. And then resolve to press on. Keep doing what you know is right because you believe the Lord will honor your faithfulness. You will accomplish incredible things through his power. Pray and press on.

III. As we persevere in the Lord's work, we can expect the world's threats. Now, we continue the story in Verse 7: *Now it happened that when Sanballat, Tobiah, the Arabs, the Ammonites, and the Ashdodites heard that the repair of the walls of Jerusalem went on, and that the places broken down began to be closed, they were very angry.* So Nehemiah and his workers committed themselves to pressing on despite the ridicule. Note the reaction of God's enemies: They were furious that the work continued. The Israelites' adversaries escalated their efforts because they used to be only Sanballat and Tobiah, who led provinces to the north of Jerusalem. However, now we read about several others, including the Arabs, who formed the tribes south of Jerusalem, the Ammonites east of Jerusalem, and the Ashdodites west of Jerusalem, not far from the modern-day Gaza Strip.

What started as ridicule from a handful of adversaries north of Jerusalem, we now read about an angry mob that surrounded Jerusalem on the north, south, east, and west. The numbers were increasing, and the rage was rising. Look at Verse 8: *All of them joined together to come and fight against Jerusalem and to cause a disturbance in it.* When the ridicule did not work, Jerusalem's enemies turned to mob violence. They banded together to attack the workers, scatter their families, and rip down the walls. In Verse 11, they said, *They will not know or see until we come among them, kill them, and put a stop to the work.* You can hear the perverted glee in their discourse: "We are going to come. We are going to kill those workers. We will tear down their wall, and they will not even see it coming. Will it not be glorious?" They have moved from ridicule to violence.

As a result, some workers began reevaluating their participation in the rebuilding project. Look at Verse 10: *Then Judah said, "The strength of the burden bearers is failing, Yet there is much rubbish; And we ourselves are unable To rebuild the wall."* Do you see what was happening? As violence was added to the ridicule, the workers on the wall said, "Maybe they are right, and we are feeble. Perhaps the idea that we could rebuild an entire city wall is a fool's errand. Maybe we should give up." And then let us read Verse 12: *Now it happened when the Jews who lived near them came and said to us ten times, "They will come up against us from every place where you may turn."* Their concern was about the women, children, and elderly who lived in the villages outside of Jerusalem bordering the Ammonites, the Ashdodites, Tobiah, Sanballat, and all those guys. All of their able-bodied men had gone to Jerusalem to build the wall, so these villages bordering God's enemies were vulnerable. The villagers were saying, "You know what? We think our men need to come home. If that attack comes, we are completely vulnerable. We need our men back here to pick up their weapons and fight." So the workers and their families living in the villages outside of town said, "Maybe it is time for us to give up this work. Maybe we should pack it up and go home." Their resolve was beginning to crumble under the withering opposition from God's enemies.

According to psychologists, this reaction to a physical threat is entirely normal. Studies show that personal threats can cause confusion, anxiety, shame, guilt, a sense of powerlessness, and more. The long-term consequences of living under threats can lead to depression, substance abuse, and chronic pain. These consequences are precisely what all of these workers were beginning to experience. The ridicule was terrible enough, but to know their very lives and property were at stake, they were starting to feel enough anxiety to reconsider the work. But you know, friends, as believers, we do not need to succumb to those emotions because we have all the necessary resources to persevere, even under the worst circumstances.

Let us look at how Nehemiah handled this latest challenge. At the beginning of Verse 9, he said, *But we prayed to our God.* Are you starting to understand that Nehemiah was a man of prayer? Recall when he first learned of the plight of God's people in Israel: His first response was fasting and prayer. And then, when he went to King Artaxerxes to ask permission to help the people of Jerusalem, he prayed throughout the entire conversation. Remember, he sent up those brief prayers to God, even as he talked to the King. And then, as the Israelites began to build and the ridicule came, he prayed through it. The physical threats were coming, and it looked like the Jewish people were at risk of immediate invasion, but again, he prayed. Nehemiah was a man of prayer. He showed us that all God's people must be people of prayer. It is the first resource available to us in trying times: to take our circumstances before the throne of heaven and ask God, who is infinite in power and wisdom, to do what we cannot do for ourselves, to trust that God will resolve this for us. We must always go to the Lord in prayer.

Look at Nehemiah's following action in the second part of Verse 9: *But we prayed to our God, and because of them we stood a guard against them day and night.* So Nehemiah prayed, but then he also took prudent steps to ensure workers' safety. He set up a guard. Friends, prayer and concrete action are not at odds. They are meant to go together. We pray our hearts out to God, asking him to work in our situations. Then, we also take this brain that God gave us, use the wisdom we have learned from Scripture, apply it practically to the matter, and take prudent steps to navigate the situation. So, we pray to God and take prudent steps.

Nehemiah then did something else. In Verse 14, he also preached to his workers: *Then I saw their fear. And I arose and said to the nobles, the officials, and the rest of the people: "Do not fear them; remember the Lord who is great and fearsome, and fight for your brothers, your sons, your daughters, your wives, and your houses."* So Nehemiah stepped behind his pulpit, as it were, and looked into the fearful eyes of those workers. He said to them, "Are you guys afraid of Sanballat? Are you afraid of Tobiah and the army of Samaria? You are afraid of the Ammonites, the Ashtodites, and the Arabs? Do not be afraid. Remember the Lord, who is great and awesome. Remember that it does not matter how few in number you are or how weak you are, because behind you stands a God who is all-powerful."

"He is the God who created the entire universe, doing nothing but exercising his will. He spoke, and time, space, matter, and energy all came into being. He is the God who rescued the Jewish people from their enslavement in Egypt, the God who showed his power over the false gods of Pharaoh by sending the plagues. He is the God who split open the Red Sea so the Jews could escape Egypt on dry ground, and then he covered the seas over again, drowning Pharaoh's army. He is the God who raised up the pagan king who permitted the Jews to go back to Jerusalem and rebuild their walls, the God who has been with them every step of the way." So Nehemiah asked, "Are you going to fear Sanballat? Fear the Lord. Remember the one we are here serving."

Friends, Nehemiah provided the answer when we face opposition of all kinds. We pray, and then we remember our God. We remember who he is, what he is like, and how he has led us from the start of our lives until now. We remember this, gain strength from it, and have confidence that the God who began a work in us will see it through to the final day. Nehemiah wrote in Verse 14, *Do not fear them; remember the Lord who is great and fearsome.* And then He added this: *And fight for your brothers, your sons, your daughters, your wives, and your houses.* So remember the Lord and then fight for what is rightfully yours. You see, Judea was their home. They were called the Jews because they were from Judea, so they had the right to be there. It is where their loved ones were all buried, where their homes currently stood, and where their families lived that very day. So Nehemiah said to them, "No more trembling before these foes. Trust in God. He is on your side, so fight for what belongs to you. Fight for your family. Fight for your land. Build this wall, and do not stop." That is Nehemiah's sermon.

So, the Israelites pressed on once more. Having prayed and taken prudent measures to ensure their safety, and having stirred up their courage again with this sermon, they now pressed on with faith, as we read in Verse 15: *Now it happened that when our enemies heard that it was known to us, and that God had thwarted their counsel, then all of us returned to the wall, each one to his work.* The enemies of God's people somehow learned that the Jews had discovered their plot to invade. Now that the plot had been discovered, it began to unravel. Notice how Nehemiah attributed this discovery to God, not to any of their own ingenuity. He wrote that God frustrated their plan, enabling them to return to work. These people had faith in God. They prayed to him, remembered him, and then had their prayers answered by him. And now they were working again. They did not just go on in faith but also with courage.

Look at Verses 16-18: *And it happened that from that day on, half of my young men carried on the work while half of them took hold of the spears, the shields, the bows, and the breastplates; and the commanders were behind the whole house of Judah. Those who were rebuilding the wall and those who carried burdens took their load, with one hand doing the work and the other holding a weapon. As for the builders, each wore his sword girded at his side as he built while the trumpeter stood near me.* Once again, we see Nehemiah's administrative genius. He believed that God would deliver them but was also taking prudent steps to ensure everyone was safe.

Here is what Nehemiah did in these verses. First, he established himself as the commander of the entire group. He then appointed a trumpeter to stand beside him, a trumpeter who would blast out Nehemiah's military orders if they were necessary. He also organized a special unit of young men into twelve-hour shifts. Half would stand guard while the other half slept and switched places every twelve hours. Then, Nehemiah established these guidelines for everyone else. The builders would work with both hands but keep a sword strapped to their side so that they could drop their tools, pick up their weapons, and fight if the enemy came. He even planned for the helpers to hand the workers their tools, stones, and other construction implements. The helpers would hand off materials to the builders with one hand while holding a weapon with the other hand. In this way, the work of God would continue while the city also hardened itself against invaders.

Think about the courage this would have taken, knowing that all around your city, hordes of people despised you, despised your God, and wanted nothing more than to cut you down and tear down your walls to ruin the work that God was doing in Jerusalem. But then you realized the work was so important that it must continue, no matter the threats. You learned to do your job with one hand passing materials and the other wielding a sword. Or some builders could build with both hands but quickly grab their swords if needed. And the guards could stand watch for any threats on the horizon. They were building with courage now.

Furthermore, we read in Verses 19-20 about the builders' optimism: *I said to the nobles, the officials and the rest of the people, "The work is great and extensive, and we are separated on the wall far from one another. At whatever place you hear the sound of the trumpet, there gather together to us. Our God will fight for us."* As the work was going on, the workers were spread thin. So, Nehemiah developed a new strategy. He said, "I will send the trumpeter to the point of the invasion if it should come. And he will blast his trumpet right where the invasion is coming. Everybody must drop their tools and go toward the sound when that happens. In that way, we can concentrate our forces and repel the invaders." The implication was that God would fight for them, which meant victory was assured. They were optimistic about the results.

Finally, in Verses 21-22, they fought with resolve: *So we kept doing the work with half of them holding spears from dawn until the stars came out. At that time I also said to the people, "Let each man with his young man spend the night within Jerusalem so that they may be a guard for us by night and a worker by day."* Notice Verse 23, where Nehemiah set the example: *So neither I, my brothers, my young men, nor the men of the guard who followed me, none of us removed our clothes, each took his weapon even to the water.* They were so committed to this job that they would not even change clothes at night. They stayed in their work clothes and kept their weapons at their side, ready to respond to any threat immediately.

IV. Application and Conclusion. Just like the people of Nehemiah's day, we, too, have a cause. We are the people of God, and we have a cause. It is laid out in our Lord's great commission. We are to make disciples of the Lord Jesus Christ to the glory of God and the transformation of this world. Friends, it is a good cause. We are privileged to be a part of it. It begins in our households as we make disciples of our own children. However, it extends outward to our community as we work together as a local church to reach our city and surrounding towns. Then, it extends beyond this local area as we deploy our missionaries, one of whom is an overseas teaching pastor. But as we deploy our people overseas to make disciples there, we have a great mission extending from here to the ends of the Earth. Let us be sure that as we do this good work—witness, share the gospel message, and see concrete successes for our efforts—we will face the jeers of the unbelieving world. Parents: People who do not understand your actions will ridicule you for your efforts. Church members: You also will face this. As a congregation, we have faced and will continue to face angry social media posts, letters to the editor in the local newspaper, and sarcastic voicemails. It will continue.

Remember, we live in a hostile world now, and the more successful we are as a church, the more intense the opposition will grow, perhaps even rising to the level of threats to our health. Friends, we have no reason to grow timid. As 2 Timothy 1:7 says, *For God has not given us a spirit of timidity, but of power and love and self-discipline.* So we press on with my family alongside yours. We press on together in this good work by praying more fervently than ever before, praying that God will clear the way before us so that his gospel message will not be hindered. We are taking prudent measures to ensure our safety and that of our children, and we will continue doing so.

We will encourage one another with the truths of the Gospel. Romans 1:16 says, *For I am not ashamed of the gospel, for it is the power of God for salvation to everyone who believes.* Friends, we will continue this good work in faith and with courage, optimism, and resolve. Together, we will build something here worthy of the name of the Lord Jesus Christ. It will endure for our kids, their grandkids, and their grandkids after them, should the Lord tarry. We will accomplish it here together with the Lord's help.

Chapter Seven

Rebuilding Our Institutional Integrity

If we want to see the Gospel move forward, we must preserve our institutional integrity.

I. Introduction to sermon on Nehemiah 5:1-19. Some of you are old enough to remember Jim and Tammy Baker. From 1974 to 1987, the Bakers hosted a TV program called the PTL (Praise the Lord) Club. This program was so popular that it soon exploded into the PTL Network. In 1979, the Federal Communications Commission began investigating allegations that the money raised by PTL was being misappropriated. Soon, they discovered that Jim Baker had raised $350,000, which he said would go to foreign missions but instead was used to build his amusement park, Heritage USA.

The Internal Revenue Service (IRS) got involved and discovered that Baker had used $1.3 million in donor funds not for ministry purposes but to enrich himself. Then, in 1987, the IRS discovered that Jim Baker had paid Miss Jessica Hahn $279,000 in hush money to cover up an alleged assault. The scandals became too much at this point, and Jim Baker resigned in disgrace. The following year, he was indicted on eight counts of mail fraud, fifteen counts of wire fraud, and one count of conspiracy. In 1989, he was sentenced to 45 years in prison, a sentence which was drastically reduced later on.

About this time, another televangelist, Jimmy Swaggart, began to face some of his own scandals. In 1988, he was accused of consorting with a prostitute. His denomination defrocked him, and he issued a public and tearful apology. But only three years later, he was caught doing the same thing again. You might also remember Robert Tilton, a televangelist and pastor of the Word of Faith Family Church (WFFC) in Farmers Branch, Texas. When the WFFC ministry peaked in 1991, its TV program was airing in all 235 American television markets, bringing in roughly $80 million annually. However, an investigation by the American Broadcasting Company (ABC) discovered that Tilton's entire ministry was adrift. Nearly all the money he raised was not used for ministry purposes but for himself. ABC found that he was not even reading his donors' prayer letters. When the mail arrived, his staff would open the envelopes, take out the checks, deposit them promptly, and then throw the letters away. ABC found all the dumpsters filled with unread letters. Tilton's ministry collapsed after this discovery, and he and his wife divorced.

Friends, I wish I could say that all the church scandals ended after Robert Tilton, but, sadly, you know that is not the case. In just the last few years, scandals involving such well-known figures as Ravi Zacharias, Josh Duggar, Johnny Hunt, and the entire executive committee of the Southern Baptist Convention made national news, damaging the cause of Christ and his Church. I do not blame the media outlets for damaging Christ's reputation. I blame the ministries that refused to police themselves and that allowed internal corruption to take hold and become an open scandal.

Through all these scandals over the years, we have learned that the greatest threat to the Church of Christ is not from the outside but from the inside. What I mean by that is that the Church's mission will continue no matter what is happening in the world. Threats, ridicule, jeers, and persecution will not stop the forward march of Christ's Church. But what can stop our progress is internal corruption—corruption that spreads within a ministry like cancer, killing it from the inside out. We cannot be stopped from the outside, but we can be stopped from the inside.

Now more than ever, if we want to be used by God to achieve something great, we must safeguard our institutional integrity. I will repeat it: We must protect our institutional integrity. If the time should ever come, and I pray to God that it does not, but if the time should ever come that wrongdoing is committed here, then we must have the moral courage to face it head-on. We must confront the wrongdoers, put them out of the Church, and repair the damage that has been done to move forward in faithful gospel ministry.

These stories take us to Nehemiah 5. For the past several weeks, we have been watching Nehemiah and his workers rebuild the walls of Jerusalem. Nehemiah had a genuine heart for the people of God and wanted to see the whole nation revived. He understood that to restore the nation, he must first revive its capital city and rebuild its walls. So, he convinced the people of Judah to buy into this vision. They had been working to rebuild the walls and had had great success. But, of course, all of this success came at a significant personal cost, and we will learn in today's chapter that one of those costs impacted their economic well-being.

Some, like Nehemiah, were wealthy, so they were fine. However, other Israelite households were not doing as well, because they were giving so much of their time, talent, energy, and resources to the revitalization of Jerusalem when they should have been paying more attention to their homesteads. Their progress in Jerusalem was amazing, but they had not planted their crops back home, which meant they had no opportunity to grow and harvest their crops. So, there was a shortage of food and money afflicting all of the Israelite workers in Jerusalem. Poverty was striking many of the workers' households. They could not meet their families' basic needs, and this threatened their work.

Unfortunately, this situation allowed a handful of unscrupulous people to exploit the suffering workers. In Chapter 5, we will discover that a small group of wealthy Israelites decided not to help their impoverished brothers and sisters but exploited them for their own personal gain. They used this opportunity to seize the hard-working builders' homes, estates, and land and even take their sons and daughters as indentured servants. So what we had here was a God-fearing group of workers being exploited by a wealthy few. And friends, this scandal of the highest order threatened to rip apart the entire project from the inside. From our chapter today, we will see how Nehemiah was made aware of the scandal and what he did to resolve it. Let us begin in Verse 1, where we learn of the problem.

II. The greatest threat to the Church's moral integrity is not external but internal. In Verse 1, Nehemiah writes, *Then there was a great outcry of the people and of their wives against their Jewish brothers.* We saw all the progress on Jerusalem's walls in prior chapters. However, in Chapter 5, the work was grinding to a halt, and all Israelites joined their voices in a great outcry. "Outcry" is an interesting word. In Exodus 3, the very same word described the turmoil of the Jews under their enslavement to the Egyptian pharaoh. Now they were crying out again. And the seriousness of their plight was reinforced by the fact that the wives were also crying out. Up to this point in the book, the wives of these workers were in the background, but now the situation was so bad at home that they brought themselves to the forefront. They joined the voices of their husbands and their brothers, and all together, they cried out in pain over what was happening to them.

They were not crying out against a pharaoh or against Sanballat, Tobiah, the Ammonites, the Ashtodites, the Arabs, or any other hostile forces we encountered in this book. No, Verse 1 says it was against their Jewish brothers. Their own fellow Israelites were oppressing them in the same way that the pharaoh of Egypt had oppressed them in generations gone by. This situation was a problem of internal corruption in the ranks of Israel. Some Israelites were financially exploiting other Israelites, and it was causing significant damage to the revitalization project.

In Verses 2-3, we get a description of what was going on: *Now there were those who were saying, "We, with our sons and our daughters, are many; therefore let us get grain that we may eat and live." Others said, "We are mortgaging our fields, our vineyards, and our houses, that we might get grain because of the famine."* Nehemiah then writes the following in Verses 4-5: *Also there were those who were saying, "We have borrowed money for the king's tax on our fields and our vineyards. But now our flesh is like the flesh of our brothers, our children like their children. Yet behold, we are forcing our sons and our daughters to be slaves, and some of our daughters are forced into subjugation, and we have no power in our hands to help, and our fields and vineyards belong to others."*

We can see what was going on here. Because all of these Jewish workers were giving all of their time, energy, and resources to building up Jerusalem, they had neglected their own homesteads. They had no food or income, so they went to the marketplace to buy what they needed. But they had no money to buy food. As a result, a small handful of very wealthy Israelites saw this situation and said, "This is something we can profit from." Instead of looking at their beleaguered brothers and sisters and offering assistance, they said, "We can help you. Do you need money to buy food? We will extend a loan to you." But they extended the loans at exorbitant interest rates—the kind nobody could ever repay. Other Israelites needed food, not money. So the wealthy Israelites among them said, "We will give you food but only in exchange for your land. If you mortgage your property, we will extend a food allowance to you." And other wealthy Israelites said, "We will give you a loan, but, in return, we want your sons and daughters as indentured servants, and they will work off the loan."

These atrocities going on in Israel at the time were a financial scandal of the highest order. Verse 7 specifies that the Jewish nobles and officials were perpetrating these crimes—the leaders of Israel. Such nobles should have been most concerned for the people's well-being. However, they were exploiting their people, the same group of people Nehemiah 3:5 said would not stoop to help in the Lord's work. So, when the work of rebuilding the walls began, these nobles and officials would not help build the walls. They said, "That is beneath us. We are not getting our hands dirty." So all these other households were doing the work and impoverishing themselves because of their devotion, while the nobles were stepping in and saying, "Oh, we can help you. And all it is going to cost you is your home, your field, your son, and your daughter. But we will help you."

My friends, this situation was a moral outrage. It was one that the Law of Moses in Exodus 22:25 explicitly addressed: *If you lend money to My people, to the afflicted among you, you are not to act as a creditor to him; you shall not charge him interest.* The Law said that if any fellow Israelites fell into poverty, you could loan them your goods and allow them to pay it back when they were able, if you wish. However, you must not provide a loan with interest to take financial advantage of their plight.

Leviticus 25:35-37 provides further guidance about this issue: *Now if a brother of yours becomes poor and his means with regard to you falter, then you are to sustain him, like a sojourner or a foreign resident, that he may live with you. Do not take usurious interest from him, but fear your God, that your brother may live with you. You shall not give him your silver at interest nor your food for gain.* This passage warned, "Don't you dare extend him loans at exorbitant interest rates to take advantage of a fellow Israelite's plight." This warning was the Law of Moses.

And then Deuteronomy 23:20 emphasizes this principle even further: *You may charge interest to a foreigner, but to your brother you shall not charge interest, so that Yahweh your God may bless you in all that you send forth your hand to do.* What was happening in Israel directly violated their most sacred laws. It also threatened the cohesion of the entire Jewish community because, if left unchecked, the exploitation of the poor would lead to social unrest, which would lead to a stoppage of the work, which would lead to the complete failure of Israel's revitalization efforts.

This internal corruption had the potential to stop God's work. It serves as a reminder that the greatest threat to us often will not come from the outside. It will come from the inside. Friends, our work here in this church today cannot be stopped by jeers, ridicule, threats, or even persecution from outside of us. Someone could burn down this building tomorrow, and the next day, our ministry would continue because we do not need this building for ministry, not ultimately. But what can grind everything to a halt? Internal corruption.

Suppose we have church members sinning unchecked against other church members. In that case, it can grow worse and eventually end our ministry. Has this not been the story of American Christianity for the last hundred or two hundred years? The American Church has not been undone by persecution. There has been no persecution to speak of. Our nation is the freest land in the world. However, the Church has been undone by its own failure to maintain institutional integrity. She failed to watch her life and doctrine closely. The lesson from Nehemiah 5 is that we must be vigilant to guard our integrity. And friends, if it should ever happen that wrongdoing begins to manifest here, we must be prepared to face it head-on. Now let us go to Nehemiah 5:6-13, where we learn of Nehemiah's response to this scandal.

III. When harm is done, God's people must confront the matter head-on. Verse 6 shows Nehemiah's initial reaction to what was happening: *Then I was very angry when I heard their outcry and these words.* So, the news finally reached Nehemiah that the Israelites were experiencing a major financial scandal afflicting the people of God. His first reaction was anger or righteous indignation at the nobles and officials, and, friends, this was precisely the proper first response to give.

When you hear that somebody who professes to love God shows contempt for the laws of God and the people of God, or when you hear of professing believers abusing other believers, causing them harm for personal gain, you should be righteously angry. But then, what will you do with that anger? It is right to feel it, but how do you resolve it? When you feel that kind of anger, you have a few options available. One option is to do nothing. Sadly, this response is typical among many institutional leaders. When an urgent matter is brought to their attention, their initial anger becomes overwhelmed with fear, and they start to tremble at the power of the wrongdoers. They fear losing monetary contributions or their position of influence within the church. As a result, they allow that anger to subside and their anxiety to rise. They say, "I will do nothing. Let us hope it takes care of itself. Maybe it will all disappear, and everything will be okay."

Friends, that is the response of too many leaders, but it does not make the problem disappear. It only worsens it and allows the crisis to fester until it becomes a media firestorm. Doing nothing in the face of internal wrongdoing in a church will lead to congregational splits, pastoral resignations, and public scandals that hit the newspapers. I have seen these results with my own eyes and have witnessed church leaders made aware of gut-wrenching, terrible wrongdoings and doing nothing because they were afraid of the people being accused. The church was destroyed as a result, and nothing remains but a shadow of its former existence. If you become aware of wrongdoing and feel righteous anger, do not suppress that feeling. Do what Nehemiah did. Do what leaders are supposed to do.

Look at Nehemiah 5:6-7 again: *Then I was very angry when I had heard their outcry and these words. I consulted within my own heart.* So Nehemiah got angry and took counsel with himself. He harnessed that righteous anger and channeled it into righteous action. He thought about what the right action would be and then took it. Nehemiah's response is what true leaders should do. When they are made aware of a growing scandal, they are righteously indignant, take counsel with themselves, and then follow a righteous course of action to remedy the problem.

Look what Nehemiah writes in Verse 7: *I consulted within my own heart and contended with the nobles and the officials.* The Israelites were experiencing a legal violation by the city elites, who had broken Moses's Law by taking financial advantage of the poor. Nehemiah's righteous response was to follow the legal process. He pressed charges against them and laid out the charges. He told them, "*You are exacting usury, each from his brother!*" And then he wrote, *Therefore, I held a great assembly against them.* He pressed charges and then laid out the indictment in the presence of everyone: "You are exploiting your fellow Israelites, something the law says you must not do."

Friends, a personal offense needs to be resolved privately. However, a public offense needs to be resolved in public. Anyone who sins against the public must stand before them and be held accountable, which Nehemiah did here. Notice he was standing against the nobles and officials, those people with all the money and power, but this wrong needed to be made right, so he set aside all those considerations and confronted the nobles and officials in front of everyone.

In Verse 8, Nehemiah details the nature of this moral outrage: "*We, according to our ability, have bought back our Jewish brothers who were sold to the nations; and now would you also sell your brothers that they may be sold to us?*" He said, "Look, all of us in Jerusalem are giving our time, energy, and money to bring the captives back and liberate the Jewish people. But when we bring them back, some of you are re-enslaving them. You are making their sons and daughters indentured servants, as well as taking away their land and their homes. We had to buy them back from the foreign nations, and now we have to buy them back from you."

Then, in the second half of Verse 8, Nehemiah writes, *Then they were silent and could not find a word to say.* They were convicted and knew they were in the wrong. In Verse 9, he writes, *And I said, "The thing which you are doing is not good; should you not walk in the fear of our God because of the reproach of the nations, our enemies?"* Nehemiah framed this situation as a spiritual problem. He said, "You elites thought this situation was a wise business move—people who need money and food—but it was not a wise financial move. It is a sin against God. You are showing contempt for God, his Law, and his people. You have committed a great sin."

Ultimately, what Nehemiah said here is true of all sin. Every time you and I sin against God, we are displaying contempt for God. We are also showing contempt for his Law, his people, and the reputation of his Church. This is what sin is and what sin does. So, Nehemiah confronted the nobles and officials with these truths. Then in Verse 10, he said, "You did have another option available to you. If you could not bring yourself to give in charity, you at least could have given a loan and told the people that they could pay it off when they were in a better position. There would have been no loss and no gain." They could have taken this course of action, but they did not. They chose the worst possible option.

Friends, these nobles and officials committed a great sin. They were doing the work of God's enemies and showing contempt for God's name and reputation. They were forsaking lawful options to help the poor in favor of law-breaking, thus setting themselves against their brothers and sisters, and, in the process, threatening to bring down the entire revitalization effort. They were destroying the work of God from within, doing what their enemies from the outside could not do.

Nehemiah proposed a solution in the second part of Verse 10: *Please, let us forsake this usury.* Here is the charge, here is why it is so serious, and here is the solution: Stop charging people interest. And then, in Verse 11, he said, *"Please, give back to them this very day their fields, their vineyards, their olive groves and their houses, also the hundredth part of the money and of the grain, the new wine and the oil that you are exacting from them."* He told them to give it all back.

In the New Testament, this solution is called "showing the fruits of repentance." It is not enough to give lip service to your regret. You cannot say, "I am sorry," then keep everything you took wrongfully. That is not repentance. Nehemiah said, "You need to forsake this taking of interest and show that you genuinely have godly sorrow for your actions. You need to give back everything you have taken wrongfully. Give the people their houses, fields, and all the interest you have earned on their money. Give it all to them. Everything has to go back. Look how the nobles and officials responded in Verse 12: *Then they said, "We will give it back and will require nothing from them; we will do exactly as you are saying."* It was the best resolution. They had been confronted publicly with their sin and then responded in repentance.

Notice what Nehemiah said next: *So I called the priests and made them swear that they would do according to this word.* Nehemiah was grateful for their promises but would not take them at their word. They had already proven themselves untrustworthy, so he said, "That sounds great. Let us bring in the priests. And right here, you will make a vow in front of God, the priests, and the entire congregation of Israel. You will vow to return everything you have taken." Then, in Verse 13, Nehemiah wrote, *I also shook out the front of my garment and said, "Thus may God shake out every man from his house and from his possessions who does not establish this word; even thus may he be shaken out and emptied."* So, Nehemiah pronounced a curse on anyone who broke the vow.

On this day, a scandal arose in Israel that threatened to bring down the entire nation. However, Nehemiah, as a godly leader, confronted it head-on. It mattered not to him that his opponents were rich and powerful. They needed to be dealt with, so he faced the problem head-on, laid out the charges, and did so publicly. He detailed the nature of their sins, called them to repentance, and, when they said they did repent, he outlined a process for reconciliation, and the guilty parties followed the process.

So, we end today's sermon with Verse 13, where Nehemiah writes, *And all the assembly said, "Amen!" And they praised Yahweh. Then the people did according to this word.* Those unscrupulous, wealthy Israelites did as they had promised. My friends, if our church is to maintain its moral integrity over the long haul, it will require a spiritual zeal that does not diminish and righteous indignation towards sin that never grows cold. It will take church leaders—and I am preaching to myself—who take credible accusations of wrongdoing seriously and are ready to fight the battle against the wrongdoers, no matter how much money they give and how powerful their position is in the church. It will require church leaders who are willing to lead by example to establish a healthy culture in their churches and who are eager to walk the talk. This leadership is what we see in Verses 14-19.

IV. After the injustice has been corrected, God's people must work to cultivate a new institutional culture. Nehemiah 5:14-19 set up Nehemiah's new institutional culture based on giving to the poor instead of taking from them and emphasizing volunteerism rather than a transactional view of every relationship. He set a new culture for Israel. We need leaders who are willing to set that culture.

V. Final applications. My friends, we should commit to this kind of institutional culture together for the glory of God and the advancement of his Church. Let it never be said that we allowed internal corruption to halt the Lord's work. Let us care about integrity. And if it should ever be threatened, may we always be committed to face it head-on, as God would have us to do.

Chapter Eight

Rebuilding with Unbreakable Leadership

If we would be used of God to achieve something great, we must build a generation of unbreakable leaders.

I. Introduction to sermon on Nehemiah 6:1–7:4. Ronald Heifetz and Marty Linsky wrote a book entitled *Leadership on the Line: Staying Alive Through the Dangers of Leadership*. It is considered one of the great books in leadership and management. I want to begin by reading an excerpt from the Introduction: "Every day the opportunity for leadership stands before you. . . . And every day you must decide whether to put your contribution out there, or keep it to yourself to avoid upsetting anyone, and get through another day. You are right to be cautious. Prudence is a virtue. You disturb people when you take unpopular initiatives in your community, put provocative new ideas on the table in your organization, question the gap between colleagues' values and behavior, or ask friends and relatives to face up to tough realities. You risk people's ire and make yourself vulnerable. Exercising leadership can get you into a lot of trouble."

Then they went on: "To lead is to live dangerously because when leadership counts, when you lead people through difficult change, you challenge what people hold dear—their daily habits, tools, loyalties, and ways of thinking—with nothing more to offer perhaps than a possibility. Moreover, leadership often means exceeding the authority you are given to tackle the challenge at hand. People push back when you disturb the personal and institutional equilibrium they know. And people resist in all kinds of creative and unexpected ways that can get you taken out of the game: pushed aside, undermined, or eliminated. It is no wonder that when the myriad opportunities to exercise leadership call, you often hesitate. Anyone who has stepped out on the line, leading part or all of an organization, a community, or a family, knows the personal and professional vulnerabilities. However gentle your style, however careful your strategy, however sure you may be that you are on the right track, leading is risky business."

Of course, no one knew better and understood the perils of leadership better than Nehemiah. If you are joining us for the first time, Nehemiah was an Israelite who lived in Persia about 2,500 years ago. He served as the cupbearer to King Artaxerxes but was also a godly man. When he learned of the distressing conditions that the children of Israel were under back in the Holy Land, he knew he had to do something, so he began to pray, fast, and brainstorm how God might use him to revitalize this chosen nation. Finally, he devised a plan to take to his boss, King Artaxerxes: He asked permission to leave Persia and return to Israel to help with its national revitalization. King Artaxerxes granted him permission, and Nehemiah returned to Jerusalem, a 750-mile journey away from Susa, where he was stationed.

Nehemiah understood that if the nation of Israel were to be revitalized, it would need to begin with its capital city in Jerusalem. And if Jerusalem were to be revitalized, it would start with rebuilding its walls. The city would forever be vulnerable if they were not rebuilt, so Nehemiah took the lead in this great effort. He mobilized all of Judah's able-bodied people and organized them to rebuild the walls of Jerusalem. We have been reading about the progress made on these walls for several weeks and have witnessed the cost of leadership. Nehemiah faced ridicule, threats, and internal scandals. However, by God's grace, he kept the project moving forward.

In today's text, Nehemiah faced still more troubles but was not deterred. He kept working on the walls and finished them. Nothing and no person could stop him in this effort. For instance, as we look at Chapters 6 and 7 together, I want us all to take away a big idea: If God uses us to achieve something great, the way Nehemiah was used in his day, we must become unbreakable leaders and raise a generation of unbreakable leaders to follow after us. But what does it mean to be an unbreakable leader? Well, friends, using today's passage as our guide, we will find that unbreakable leaders have at least four virtues. The first is found in Nehemiah 6:1-4.

II. Unbreakable leaders are willing to be despised. The first virtue of unbreakable leaders is that they are willing to be hated and despised by the unbelieving world. Of course, they do not want to be despised and are not seeking to be despised. They would be pleased if everybody liked them. However, unbreakable leaders are willing to endure the world's hostility as the price they must pay to keep God's work moving forward. Let us look at Verses 1-2 and read about this virtue: *Now it happened when it was heard by Sanballat, Tobiah, Geshem the Arab, and the rest of our enemies that I had rebuilt the wall, and that no breach remained in it, although at that time I had not made the doors to stand in the gates, that Sanballat and Geshem sent a message to me, saying, "Come, let us meet together at Chephirim in the plain of Ono."*

We see what was happening here. Nehemiah was leading this building effort, and the work was near completion. The walls were up, and all that remained was putting in the gates. Nehemiah's adversaries were nervous because they realized Jerusalem would be difficult to penetrate once the gates were in, so they knew they were running out of time. If they were going to stop this project, they realized they must stop it immediately. However, so far, the jeering, ridiculing, and threatening failed to work, so they would need to use a new strategy: They would call for a meeting between them and Nehemiah in Hakepharim in the plain of Ano, about 30 miles northwest of Jerusalem, which was hostile territory for Nehemiah. I am sure their invitation was very diplomatic and probably went something like this: "Listen, Nehemiah, we have been at loggerheads for a while now. You have your ideas and we have ours, but we have not reached an understanding. So, let us meet together in the plains of Ano and hash out our differences; we no longer have to be enemies." Yet Nehemiah knew there were ulterior motives here because the end of Verse 2 said, *But they were planning to do me harm.*

As innocent as their invitation may have sounded, Nehemiah knew the actual intent: They were trying to get him out of Jerusalem's safety and into their territory, where he would almost certainly be captured or killed. Because Nehemiah was the driving force behind the rebuilding efforts, the project would surely grind to a halt if he were removed. Their plan was yet another effort to stop the revitalization of Jerusalem. We see Nehemiah's response in Verse 3: *So I sent messengers to them, saying, "I am doing a great work and I cannot come down. Why should the work stop while I leave it and come down to you?"* I am sure Nehemiah was diplomatic about the wording of his message. He said to them, "Listen, guys. I know you would love to meet with me and try to hash out our differences, but you must understand we are at a critical stage of this building project, and I cannot get away. I need to stay here in Jerusalem." Then he got back to work.

In Verse 4, we now see the enemy's desperation: *And they sent messages to me four times in this manner, and I responded to them in the same manner.* Nehemiah's enemies realized there was no other way to stop the rebuilding effort. Nothing they tried had worked. The only plan left was to get Nehemiah out of Jerusalem's safety and into their territory, where they could take him out. When Nehemiah said no the first time, they came back to him repeatedly and tried to wear him down with their requests. In Verse 5, Nehemiah continued to rebuff their invitations: *Then Sanballat sent his young man to me in the same manner a fifth time with an open letter in his hand.* So this time, they emphasized the same strategy but with a different tactic: They came to Nehemiah with an open letter that would be read to all of Jerusalem's residents to influence public opinion against him.

Friends, being a leader of God's people is an unspeakable privilege, but it also has a dark side to it. We are witnessing the dark side right here, because if there is opposition to God's work and you are the one leading that work, then all that hostility will be directed at you, and it will come at you repeatedly. If you aspire to spiritual leadership, whether at home, in the local church, or in the community, you must learn how to cope with hostility and people jeering at you, threatening you, and plotting to do you harm, maybe even wishing that you were dead. You must learn how to live with these threats.

How does one learn to cope with it? Here is what I suggest: We cope by learning how to value the approval of God more than the approval of godless men. That is all there is to it. We must learn to prioritize God's pleasure, have a big view of God, and make his pleasure our driving ambition. If we can say, "My driving ambition is to enter the presence of God and hear from his lips, 'Well done, good and faithful servant,'" then whether people approve or disapprove of us will become immaterial. Of course, we would rather be liked and praised by our fellow man, but if those worldly desires come at the cost of that joyful meeting with God, where he says to us, "Well done," then we, as unbreakable leaders, must be willing to give up such desires. Friends, learning to value God's approval over man's approval is the key to persevering in leadership when the enemies of God seek to do you harm. Unbreakable leaders are willing to be despised. That is the first virtue of unbreakable leadership. We now turn to the second virtue.

III. Unbreakable leaders do not give in to fear. Fear is a theme that runs throughout our text today. We have already read that Sanballat, for the fifth time, sent an open letter, but now let us look at what the letter says in Verses 6 and 7: *In it was written, "It is heard among the nations, and Gashmu says, that you and the Jews are planning to rebel; therefore you are rebuilding the wall. And you are to be their king, according to these words. You have also set up prophets to call out in Jerusalem concerning you, 'A king is in Judah!' So now it will be heard by the king according to these words. So now, come, let us take counsel together."*

So four times, Sanballat, Tobiah, Geshem, and all of these other adversaries sent letters to Nehemiah that invited him to come to Ono for a meeting. He said no every time. They were using the same strategy but with a new scheme: They sent an open letter as a fear tactic. It said, "You know, Nehemiah, rumor has it that you are so determined to finish the city walls because you intend to use Jerusalem as the launching point for a rebellion against Persia. There is also a rumor that you have prophets in Jerusalem declaring you as the rightful king. We sure would hate for this rumor to get back to King Artaxerxes. If he heard about it, you know what would happen. It would not just be you who was killed, but every man, woman, and child in Judah would be wiped off the map. You do not want that to happen, do you?" They tried to instill fear in the Israelites, as written in Verse 9: *For all of them were trying to frighten us, thinking, "Their hands will become limp in doing the work, and it will not be done."* This fear tactic reappears in Verses 13, 14, and 19. When they could not get Nehemiah to them by one means, they tried another: fear. They wanted to make Nehemiah and the people of Jerusalem afraid.

Friends, what is fear? It is the body's natural response to real or perceived threats, functioning as a powerful emotion. When you are afraid, stress hormones like cortisol and adrenaline course through your body. Your blood pressure and heart rate increase, you breathe faster, and your fight-or-flight instinct kicks in. Remaining in a state of fear for an extended period can weaken your immune system and cause cardiovascular damage, migraines, gastrointestinal problems, decreased fertility, accelerated aging, and even premature death. These symptoms are what chronic fear does to a person, which is why God's enemies often resort to fear tactics; fear is unpleasant.

If you can stoke fear in a person and sustain it over the long haul, it wears down your body. You might get to a point where you can no longer bear to feel this way. It affects your health and everything else in your life, so you want it to go away. If not controlled, fear can lead you to do things you would never otherwise do, like violate your conscience or even give up your life's calling. That is what Nehemiah's enemies tried to accomplish: Make him afraid. They wanted him to not only fear the loss of his own life, but to make him think that if he continued this course of action, he could cost the lives of all of the people he loved and all the people he was laboring for, as well as cause all of Israel's hopes to come crashing down.

How did Nehemiah handle these fear tactics? We see three responses in Verses 8-9. First, he called out the lies, as written in Verse 8: *Then I sent a message to him, saying, "Such words as you are saying have not been done, but you are devising them in your own heart."* So Nehemiah's adversaries came with an open letter, which was read at a public hearing. Nehemiah, who had to respond to the charges in public, declared in the hearing of all, "You are liars. We are not rebuilding Jerusalem because we want to rebel against Persia. I am not declaring myself any kind of king. No, this is just about restoring our ancient home. We want our home again."

Second, in Verse 9, he prayed for courage: *For all of them were trying to frighten us, thinking, "Their hands will become limp in doing the work, and it will not be done."* Notice how he pivoted to prayer: *But now, O God, strengthen my hands.* All of this opposition to Nehemiah was beginning to wear on him. His hands may have been growing a bit shaky, so, as this latest attempt to stop the work came his way, he stopped and prayed to God: "God, make me courageous again. Please help me keep working, even with all this opposition coming my way." So Nehemiah called out the lies and prayed to God for courage. And then, friends, his third response was to keep on working. He kept on going.

Listen, my friends, we cannot give people the power to make us afraid. That is doubly true for those of us who would like to be spiritual leaders because, as a leader, you will be confronted with some frightening things, whether you are a Christian mom, dad, employer, deacon, pastor, or organizational leader. You must not give people the power to make you so afraid that you give up the good work that God would have you do. When those times come, you must take your stand. But how do we overcome the fear of man? The answer is we overcome it with the fear of God.

And I am talking about a healthy kind of fear. The people around us—their opinions, threats, strategies, tactics, and all of that—will be less threatening to us if we have a big view of God. If you see God in all his glory, majesty, power, and dominion, you will see humans for what they are: small and powerless. What is the worst they can do to us? Scriptures say they can kill the body, but they cannot kill the everlasting soul. We have no reason to fear men if we have a healthy fear of God. If your view of God is big enough, every threat that comes your way from godless people will suddenly look like an ant shaking its fist at you and saying, "How dare you do God's work!" You will not be afraid if your God is big.

Another thing that can take away fear is your assurance of living in a state of grace. The prospect of death can be frightening if you are unsure what will happen to you after you depart from this world. The anxiety over death comes from not knowing our standing with God. That fear can be removed if you are in a state of grace. Make sure you have approached God through Jesus Christ in repentant faith; trusted wholeheartedly in his life, death, and resurrection; and been counted among his disciples. Suppose people suddenly threaten you with even the worst they can do. In that case, it will not be overpowering when you have the assurance of eternal life in heaven. My friends, we need unbreakable leaders today who are willing to be despised by the world and not cave to fear. And thirdly, we also need leaders who are not deterred by the pain of betrayal.

IV. Unbreakable leaders are not deterred by the pain of betrayal. Look at Nehemiah 6:10 with me: *Now I entered the house of Shemaiah, the son of Delaiah, son of Mehetabel, who was confined at home, and he said, "Let us meet together in the house of God, within the temple, and let us close the doors of the temple, for they are coming to kill you, and they are coming to kill you at night."* Who was Shemaiah? He was a prophet and perhaps a temple priest; therefore, he was a fellow Jew living in Jerusalem and confined to his home, probably because of some ritual uncleanness. But why would Shemaiah suggest that he and Nehemiah hide in the Temple to run from the threats of Israel's enemies? We start to understand what was happening here when we look at Nehemiah's response in Verse 11: *But I said, "Should a man like me flee?"* Nehemiah said, "Do you want me to run away? How can I run away? I am the leader of this effort. What will happen to all the workers if I run away? They will run away, too, and the work will stop. You would not want me to bring the whole project to a halt, would you? You are a religious leader and one of us, are you not? You would not want me to do that."

Nehemiah continued in the second part of Verse 11: *"And could one such as I go into the temple just to live? I will not go in."* He said, "Listen, besides all that, I am not a prophet, nor a priest. I have no right to enter the Temple. If I enter, God could rightly strike me dead, so either way, I am a dead man. If I keep working, you say they will kill me. If I enter the Temple, God will kill me. I might as well continue doing the work of God on the city walls and stay right where I am. I am a dead man either way." But here is where the story takes an unfortunate turn, as written in Verses 12-13: *Then I recognized that surely God had not sent him, but he spoke his prophecy against me because Tobiah and Sanballat had hired him. He was hired for this reason, that I might become afraid and act accordingly and sin, so that they could give me a bad name in order that they could reproach me.*

You know, friends, of all the challenges a leader must face, none is more painful than dealing with betrayal. You have one or more people who have pledged themselves to the same cause as you, proclaimed their loyalty to you, and labored alongside you, maybe for a long time. You pour your hearts into one another and do God's work together. But then, through no fault of your own, they turn on you unexpectedly. Suddenly, someone who is your friend becomes your enemy. The one person who works for the same cause is now trying to cause others to oppose you.

Friend, nothing is worse than betrayal. Has it ever happened to you? In your family? At work? I hope not in church. But has it ever happened to you? Perhaps someone vowed to love and cherish you, and suddenly turned against you. Or maybe some people you had personally led to Christ became a part of your church family. You thought you saw spiritual growth in their lives, but suddenly, they came to you and said, "Guess what? You are now my enemy." And they walked away, leaving you demoralized. Nothing is worse than experiencing this. That is what happened to Nehemiah.

A religious leader in Jerusalem had been with Nehemiah all this time. Now, he was suddenly doing the work of Nehemiah's enemies, trying to get him to stop building the walls. He turned on Nehemiah. How did Nehemiah get past this betrayal? How does anyone get past the pain of betrayal? Well, look at his prayer in Verse 14: *Remember, O my God, Tobiah and Sanballat according to these works of theirs, and also Noadiah the prophetess and the rest of the prophets who were trying to make me afraid.* He said, "Remember these things they did in turning my own people against me." So we learn for the first time that his betrayal was not the result of just one religious leader. There was a whole gaggle of these people turning against him. Nehemiah was now facing an entire cohort that treated him as an enemy; all he could do was pray about it.

My friend, when you face a great betrayal, the best action is to get on your knees and hand off the pain to God, and then remember these truths: Your commission, whatever it is—dad, mom, church member, deacon, pastor—is a job that you have through the commission of God. It does not come from man. Remember that God will never leave nor forsake you. Everybody else might turn from you, but he never will. Also, remember that God never asks you to endure anything he has not been willing to endure himself. God knows what it is like to be betrayed. Lucifer, now called the devil and perhaps the most glorious of all of God's created beings, betrayed him and took many angels with him. And then, in the Garden of Eden, after God built a perfect paradise for Adam and Eve and walked with them in the garden, they turned against him and became his enemies. Think of our Lord Jesus Christ, how one of his best friends, a man named Judas, was the one who turned him over to the authorities and had him crucified. God knows what it is like to be betrayed, so we continue on. We press past the hostility of the godless world and never succumb to its fear tactics. Painful betrayals will not stop us. Now we will discuss a fourth virtue.

V. Unbreakable leaders learn to live in a state of peril. This point is a combination of the previous three virtues. To live with peril means you know how to live with hostility, fear, betrayal, and threats. You learn to live with them. Let us look at Verses 15-19, where Nehemiah writes, *So the wall was finished on the twenty-fifth of the month Elul, in fifty-two days.* So he did it. He pressed past everything against him and completed the walls, the gates, all of it. And in Verse 16, we read, *Now it happened that when all our enemies heard of it, and all the nations surrounding us saw it, their confidence fell. And they knew that it was from our God that this work had been accomplished.* So all this time, Nehemiah's enemies tried to make him afraid, but he pressed past it. And look at what happened: A significant reversal took place. The enemies of Jerusalem were afraid because they were up against an unbreakable man of God who could not be deterred. They realized there was no stopping a person with God on his side.

We learn even more about these betrayals in Verses 17-19, where Nehemiah writes, *Now it happened that when all our enemies heard of it, and all the nations surrounding us saw it, their confidence fell. And they knew that it was from our God that this work had been accomplished. Also in those days many letters went from the nobles of Judah to Tobiah, and Tobiah's letters came to them. For many in Judah were sworn by oath to him because he was the son-in-law of Shecaniah the son of Arah, and his son Jehohanan had taken the daughter of Meshullam the son of Berechiah as a wife. Moreover, they were speaking about his good deeds in my presence and bringing my words to him. Then Tobiah sent letters to make me afraid.* Now we understand how all of these betrayals took place. There were family connections between Israel's wealthy and influential citizens, like the religious leaders and nobles, and the rich and powerful people of Israel's surrounding nations, like Sanballat and Tobiah. There were family connections between these groups and exchanges of letters between them. Tobiah and Sanballat sent letters to Israel, and those families sent letters back. These connections were how they maintained their communication and how the people in Jerusalem were able to turn against Nehemiah.

But he continued to live with it and kept pressing on. In Nehemiah 7:1-4, we read the following about what happened in Jerusalem after the walls and gates were rebuilt: *Now it happened when the wall was rebuilt and I had made the doors to stand, and the gatekeepers and the singers and the Levites were appointed, that I commanded Hanani my brother and Hananiah the commander of the fortress, to be over Jerusalem, for he was a faithful man and feared God more than many. Then I said to them, "The gates of Jerusalem must not be opened until the sun is hot; and until they are there standing guard, they must shut and bolt the doors. Also have guards from the inhabitants of Jerusalem stand, each at his post, and each in front of his own house." Now the city was large and spacious, but the people in it were few and the houses were not rebuilt.* The walls were finished, the real revitalization was beginning, and the restoration of Jerusalem's worship was at hand. However, life in Jerusalem was still very dangerous, with few residents, a big city to watch over, and the need to build family homes. In response, Nehemiah appointed guards to keep watch and established a curfew to get everyone behind the city walls before dark. But notice that he did not leave. He accepted the perils of leadership and remained in the city no matter what came his way.

Friends, in a summary of his book *Risk is Right*, John Piper offered this challenge: "A choice lies before you: Either waste your life or live with risk. Either sit on the sidelines or get in the game. After all, life was no cakewalk for Jesus, and he didn't promise it would be any easier for his followers. We shouldn't be surprised by resistance and persecution. Yet most of us play it safe. We pursue comfort. We spend ourselves to get more stuff. And we prefer to be entertained. We are all tempted by the idea of security, the possibility of a cozy Christianity with no hell at the end. But what kind of life is that? It's a far cry from adventurous and abundant, from truly rich and really full, and it's certainly not the heights and the depths Jesus calls us to." Piper concluded with the suggestion that we should "see the joys of a faith-filled and seriously rewarding life of Jesus-dependent abandon!" That is the need of the hour.

VI. Conclusion. We need spiritual leaders today: godly fathers, mothers, pastors, deacons, and community members. Suppose God would indeed use us in a leadership capacity. In that case, we must learn to become unbreakable, which is to say we must put on the four virtues of leadership. We must be willing to be despised by the world if that is the price to pay for us to do God's work. We must never give in to fear. The pain of betrayal must not deter us. And we must learn how to live in peril. My friends, these virtues will only become more critical in the years ahead, not less, so let us do what we must to become this kind of leader.

What steps will you take to become a leader today? What spiritual disciplines have you been neglecting that you need to start taking seriously? Parents, what must you do to raise a generation of unbreakable leaders? What kind of education do you think your children need? What level of involvement in a local church do they need? What kind of example do you need to provide for them? What opportunities do you need to give them? What adversity do you need to expose them to? What must you do to raise a new generation of spiritual leaders with unbreakable resolve? Church members, how can you help one another become the leaders we need at this hour? Let us think about these questions together.

Chapter Nine

Rebuilding Corporate Worship

Biblical reformations are fueled by biblical worship.

I. Introduction to sermon on Nehemiah 7:5–8:8. In 1961, A. W. Tozer wrote that worship is the missing jewel in the evangelical church. He said, "To great sections of the church, the art of worship has been lost entirely, and in its place has come that strange and foreign thing called the' program.' This word has been borrowed from the stage and applied with sad wisdom to the public service which now passes for worship among us." In other words, Tozer said that the evangelical church has replaced worship with amusements. I wish worship had improved in the 60 years since he wrote those words. But sadly, it has not. If anything, it has continued to worsen: Corporate worship in many churches is indistinguishable from worldly entertainment.

Friends, this sad reflection on worship is not pleasing to God. And so, it would seem that the recovery of true God-honoring worship should be a matter of first importance for the Church today, just as it was for Nehemiah in his day. If you are joining us for the first time, Nehemiah was an Israelite who lived in Persia about 2,500 years ago. He was also a very godly man. When he learned about the awful state of God's people in Israel, he knew he had to do something about it, so immediately, he began to fast, pray, and brainstorm until he finally devised a plan. He then took his plan to King Artaxerxes of

Persia. Artaxerxes permitted him to execute the plan, so Nehemiah packed his bags and traveled 750 miles to Jerusalem, where he began a rebuilding effort in Israel.

Nehemiah was brilliant. He realized that if the nation of Israel were to be revitalized, it would need to begin with its capital city, Jerusalem. He also understood that if Jerusalem were to be revitalized, it would need to start with its walls. As long as Jerusalem had no walls, the city would be vulnerable to foreign invasions. So Nehemiah marshaled a heroic effort to rebuild the city walls. For several weeks, we watched him lead this effort, getting all of Israel involved—men, women, and children. The walls had been completed, so the question was: What would Nehemiah do next? The answer is that he set out to rebuild Israel's worship because only God-honoring worship can achieve lasting reformation or revitalization. Reformations are fueled by worship.

Today's text is rather lengthy but breaks up very nicely into two main parts. In Chapter 7, we see Nehemiah's preparations for worship. Then, in the first part of Chapter 8, we see Jerusalem's first corporate worship service. I will go through Chapter 7 quickly so we can spend most of our time in the opening verses of Chapter 8. Let us begin with Chapter 7 as we read about Nehemiah's preparations for worship.

II. Corporate worship is a matter of first importance. How did Nehemiah prepare God's people for worship? He conducted a census and attributed the idea to God himself. Look at Verse 5 with me: *Then my God put it into my heart, and I gathered the nobles, the officials, and the people to be recorded by genealogies.* What was Nehemiah doing here? He wanted to find out how many people were in Israel, to what tribes they all belonged, and where they all lived. However, he was also concerned with identifying who could lead their corporate worship.

In Verse 43, he identified all of the Levites, the tribe responsible for leading Israel's worship. In Verse 44, he identified all the singers who would play a crucial role in worship. In Verse 45, he identified all the gatekeepers responsible for worship. In Verse 46, he identified all the temple servants who would assist the priests in worship. Then, in Verse 57, he identified all the sons of Solomon's servants, who were still helpers in worship. In Verse 60, he identified additional temple servants.

Then we come to Verses 63-65. This passage is fascinating because Nehemiah identified a group of men claiming to be Israelites. They desired to serve as priests in Israel but could not prove their biblical qualifications. So, Nehemiah denied their request. His response was essential because he was desperate to restart Israel's worship. Still, he could not do so at the expense of biblical faithfulness. He needed priests, but if these men could not prove that they were biblically qualified to serve as priests, he could not allow them to serve. This section teaches us the importance of regulating our worship according to the Scriptures.

Now, we come to Verses 70-72. After completing the census and finding out who could lead worship, Nehemiah raised money to restart the worship services, beginning with himself. Look at Nehemiah 7:70-71 with me: *Some from among the heads of fathers' households gave to the work. The governor gave to the treasury 1,000 gold drachmas, 50 bowls, 530 priests' tunics. Some of the heads of fathers' households gave into the treasury of the work 20,000 gold drachmas and 2,200 silver minas.* This donation was massive. It shows us how committed Nehemiah was to restarting Israel's worship.

I have done the math on this chapter, and the average donation was about one drachma of gold for every man, woman, and child in Israel. But Nehemiah donated 1,000 drachmas of gold on his own—again, a considerable donation. He also donated utensils and garments, which the priests would use to lead worship. Verse 73 concludes Nehemiah's preparations: *So the priests, the Levites, the gatekeepers, the singers, some of the people, the temple servants, and all Israel lived in their cities. Then the seventh month came, and the sons of Israel were in their cities.* Nehemiah had a good picture of what was going on in Israel. He knew how many people there were—a little over 40,000. He also knew who was available for worship and who qualified as priests, temple servants, singers, gatekeepers, and everyone else. Nehemiah successfully raised all the funds needed to make the worship service happen.

Now, we turn to Chapter 8:1-8 and witness Israel's first public worship service since Nehemiah's return. Friends, as we walk through these verses together, I want to draw your attention to six features of that first worship service because these features ought to be present in every worship service, at every time, and in every place. They should be present here every time we gather. Let us examine the first of them together.

III. God-pleasing corporate worship will be filled with eager participants. Nehemiah 8:1 shows that a God-honoring worship service will be filled with eager participants. Look at Verse 1 with me: *And all the people gathered as one man at the square which was in front of the Water Gate, and* *they said to Ezra the scribe to bring the book of the law of Moses which Yahweh had commanded to Israel.* Notice the language at the start of this verse: The congregation of Israel gathered *as one man*. That means men, women, and children gathered for this singular purpose and with one desire: to worship God together as a congregation.

In the second part of Verse 2, Nehemiah writes that *men, women, and all who could understand when listening* gathered in this great assembly. There were men, women, children, families, the elderly, and the very young, making it a multi-generational, family-integrated event. Verse 1 also indicates that this massive congregation told Ezra to come and lead their worship. So, the initiative came from the congregation. They said to Ezra, "We have gathered together. We want to worship God and need someone to lead us." The end of Verse 3 indicates that *all the ears of the people were attentive to the book of the law* as Ezra spoke.

Friends, this congregation is a model for all congregations at all times. We ought to be eager every time we gather to worship and be as enthusiastic as these Israelites were at their first opportunity to worship God corporately. If you ever struggle to find the motivation to get up and join with the people of God in corporate worship, let me offer you one simple suggestion: Take a moment to ponder the privilege of corporate worship. Think of all that God has done in your life. You were once alienated from God and hostile in mind, but now, God, in his grace, has done a work inside of you. He took your heart of stone, softened it, and made it a heart of flesh. He also took your mind, which was hostile to God, and removed the barriers. And by his spiritual enablement, you became willing to believe and bow before him as your Lord. God redeemed you. In his grace, he brought a gospel messenger—maybe a pastor, a Christian family member, or a friend—but he brought the Gospel to you. And by his grace, you heard the Gospel, believed, and were born again. At that moment, you ceased to be an enemy of God and became one of his children. God did that for you.

The amazing part is he has not done that for only you but for many other people in the same vicinity where you live. In his providence, God has allowed all of you—his redeemed people, his children—to come together as a single congregation. You have the high privilege of gathering with your fellow saints on the first day of the week, every week, to praise God for all he is and all he has done for every one of you. Friends, could there be a greater privilege? The week's highlight should be to gather with those people God has saved, our new spiritual family, and have fellowship and worship him together.

God is honored by an eager congregation of worshipers. The congregation in Israel was there to worship him, and we should be as well. God-honoring worship is filled with enthusiastic participants. We then see a second feature of God-honoring worship: A biblically qualified man will lead it.

IV. God-pleasing corporate worship will be led by a biblically qualified man. We have already noted how Nehemiah excluded a group of men who wanted to lead worship but were not qualified. So then, who did they get to lead their worship? Nehemiah 8:1 tells us that it was a man called *Ezra the scribe*. Who was he? Well, friends, in Ezra 7:1-6, his qualifications are listed out for us. First, Ezra was a direct descendant of Aaron, the high priest, so he had a biblical lineage to serve in the priesthood. Second, Ezra 7:6 states that he was deeply knowledgeable of the Scriptures. Thirdly, Ezra 7:6 states that *the hand of Yahweh his God was upon him*, so he was spiritually zealous, a pious man who allowed God to work in his life. In short, Ezra was a pastor scholar par excellence. He loved God's Word, loved God's people, and studied hard to lead the worship. He was fit to lead the congregation on this momentous day in Jerusalem.

Friend, Ezra was the kind of man we need today. We do not need men with good looks, excellent guitar-playing skills, or winning personalities. We need men who have studied long and hard to know God's Word today to lead our worship services, men who have devoted years of their lives to familiarizing themselves with the content of Scriptures, and who know the storyline of the Bible from start to finish. We need men who have learned how the storyline of Scripture fits into a coherent worldview, who know their systematic theology and church history, and who understand the languages and culture of the Bible. We need men who know how to take the timeless truths of Scripture and apply them to the everyday lives of God's people.

We also need men of proven virtue who are not interested in the job because they think they can acquire power, fame, or riches but are committed to righteousness, holiness, and moral goodness. We need men of proven righteousness whom God has transformed through the Scriptures and who have experienced God's leading in their lives, men who can speak to God's people out of their own experience. These kinds of men are needed to lead God's worship today, and there is an extreme shortage of such men. So, let me speak to the young men of our congregation right now.

Young men, if you feel a stirring within you to lead God's people, do not suppress it. Let me encourage you to cultivate it because we need qualified men. As you look at the pastoral epistles in our New Testament and compare them to your life, and say, "Look, I know I do not fully measure up yet, but I think I meet the basic requirements here of the Scriptures to lead God's people," then continue to work at that. And young men and boys, let me encourage you to come to me or our associate pastor and tell us about this growing desire. I was only ten years old when I went to the associate pastor of my church and said, "I want to be a pastor. Can you help me?" He started to meet with me, and we went through the virtues required for the pastorate, one at a time, as a ten-year-old boy. It is never too early to start.

Friends, there is a shortage of qualified men, so please consider the pastorate yourself. Yes, it is a long process and difficult. Before your ordination, there is much to learn, but you will have all the help you need at every step. Here at our church, you will have me and our associate pastor to help you through the process. We will get you the resources needed to pay for your schooling. We will mentor you and give you the opportunities needed to gain experience. We will help you with our congregation to decide whether you are truly qualified for the work. My friends, God-honoring worship is filled with eager participants and led by biblically qualified men. Now, let us look at the third feature of God-honoring worship.

V. God-pleasing corporate worship will be centered on God's Word. What does it mean for a worship service to be centered on God's Word? It means that God's Word will be the only Word offered. Look at Nehemiah 8:1 again with me: *And they said to Ezra the scribe to bring the book of the law of Moses which Yahweh had commanded to Israel.* So, this congregation gathered and was ready to worship. They wanted Ezra to come and lead it, saying, "Ezra, we want you to bring the book." And they called it *the book of the law of Moses*, another way to reference the Pentateuch, the first five books of the Bible. They said, "Ezra, come, lead us in worship. And when you do, bring the Scriptures. We want to hear the Scriptures." In Nehemiah 8:1, the book was called the book *which Yahweh had commanded to Israel.*

That is why the Scriptures must be central to our worship; the Scriptures do not record the words of mere men. No, these are the words of God. They are inspired, inerrant, and infallible words. Friends, when we gather for worship, we do not need a word from the local newspaper columnist, the latest pop psychology text, or the preacher's funny anecdotes. We need to hear from God's Word because his Word has the words of everlasting life. John Calvin wrote to his fellow pastors: "When we enter the pulpit, it is not so that we may bring our own dreams and fancies with us." He believed the minister's whole task was limited to the ministry of the Word.

Friends, a God-centered worship service begins with God's Word, concludes with God's Word, and every part of the service is informed by God's Word. The hymns and prayers reflect biblical truth. The Scriptures are read verbatim to the congregation, and the sermon is derived from God's Word. Every bit of it is from God's Word and no other place. Another element of worship that centers on God's Word is that his Word will be expounded for an extended period of time, which we see in 8:2-3, where Nehemiah writes, *Then Ezra the priest brought the law before the assembly of men, women, and all who could understand when listening, on the first day of the seventh month. And he read from it before the square which was in front of the Water Gate from early morning until midday.*

Notice that Ezra read God's Word *from early morning until midday.* For half a day, he read and expounded the Scriptures, and he did so *in the presence of the men and the women, those who could understand, and all the ears of the people were attentive to the book of the law.* Friends, when we gather for corporate worship, we need an extended time in God's Word. It need not be half a day, like on this occasion in Jerusalem. However, it must be long enough for a meaningful exposition of the text so that everyone who attends the worship service can leave that day saying, "I now understand a portion of the Scriptures that I never understood before. I know its context and its interpretation. I know how it applies to my life." The exposition must be long enough so everyone can leave saying those comments.

As the Puritan minister Richard Bernard put it, "Preaching is not a labor of the lips, and an idle talk of the tongue from a light imagination of the mind; but is indeed an uttering of God's truth from a serious meditation of the heart, in sound judgment, acquired through God's blessing by diligent labor and study to profit God's people. This preaching is of worth, deserves esteem, procures credit to God's ordinance, will work upon the hearers, and will pierce deeply, as being spoken with authority." You see, time spent in God's Word should occur only after the speaker has given hours to study, and the people hearing the message should study the Word, too, so they leave knowing the Scriptures better than when they arrived.

A Word-centered service is one in which God's Word is the only foundation considered, where his Word is expounded upon for an extended period of time. We also see in Verse 4 that God's Word is delivered authoritatively: *Ezra the scribe stood on a wooden podium which they had made for the purpose.* And the word translated as "podium" here literally means a tower. Ezra spoke to more than 40,000 people, so he needed to be elevated high. He ascended a high wooden platform with a copy of the Scriptures. On this day, the Scriptures were physically elevated above the worshipers, which was by design.

The Scriptures were elevated on a platform above the worshipers, which communicated that God's Word brought the congregation together and that they were submitting themselves to the Scriptures. The one who read and expounded the Scriptures was likewise elevated so that all could hear and understand God's Word. Notice the following response from the Israelites in Verse 5: *And Ezra opened the book in the sight of all the people for he was above all the people; and when he opened it, all the people stood up.* This response from the people was a spontaneous movement of the crowd. As they saw Ezra ascend the platform with a copy of God's Word in his hand and saw the solemn way he set those Scriptures down and opened them up to read from, people realized this service was a moment of great magnitude. The seriousness with which Ezra completed his work caused everyone in the congregation to arise as if a dignitary were entering the room, except it was the Scriptures, the Word of God, coming to them. And they stood out of respect for the Word of God.

My friends, having a minister of God or a congregation take the Word of God lightly will not do for us. As the Puritan Matthew Simpson stated, The preacher's "throne is the pulpit; he stands in Christ's stead; his message is the word of God; around him are immortal souls; the Savior, unseen, is beside him; the Holy Spirit broods over the congregation; angels gaze upon the scene, and heaven and hell await the issue. What associations, and what vast responsibility." Friends, in a God-honoring worship service, the preacher and the congregation will realize that they are part of something significant: They are hearing from the authoritative Word of God, and God's Word is presented with authority. It is heard by those worshippers who have assigned authority to the Scriptures. They recognize its authority over their lives. A worship service centered on God's Word allows you to see his Word explained to be understood. We have seen the importance of understanding throughout this text, as written in Verse 2: *And all who could understand when listening gathered in this great assembly.* Verse 3 states, *Those who could understand listened intently as Ezra spoke.*

In Verses 7-8, we find something very interesting: a listing of names—Ezra's helpers. Nehemiah writes in Verses 7-8 that they *were providing understanding of the law to the people while the people stood in their place. They read from the book, from the law of God, explaining and giving insight, and they provided understanding of the reading.* Here is what was going on. Ezra was on a high platform reading and expounding God's Word. But remember, he spoke to more than 40,000 people with no speaker system, so some people could hear him, but many could not. In response, Ezra sent a group of biblically qualified assistants into the crowd. I imagine them going to the back of the crowd, repeating the Word of God that Ezra was reading, so everybody could hear the same thing. They also expounded upon the Scriptures the way Ezra did. They translated and interpreted the Scriptures and helped the people apply them to their lives. So Ezra headed a group leading the exposition of God's Word, while others walked through the crowd, reading and expositing the Scriptures. The goal was to help every worshiper hear and understand the Word of God.

Friends, corporate worship is not just a religious ritual. It is the act of God's people gathering to hear and understand his Word so they might respond in praise and obedience. And for that response to happen, the message must be clear. As Charles Spurgeon said, "However excellent your matter, if a man does not comprehend it, it can be of no use to him." God's Word must be understood as it is read and explained. So, friends, God-honoring worship is filled with eager participants, led by a biblically qualified man, and centered on God's Word, meaning that God's Word is read and expounded upon at length and held in high authority by the preacher and congregation alike. Now, let us explore another feature of God-honoring worship.

VI. God-pleasing corporate worship will be aimed at the glory of God. In 8:6, Nehemiah writes, *Then Ezra blessed Yahweh the great God. And all the people answered, "Amen, Amen!" while lifting up their hands; then they bowed low and worshiped Yahweh with their faces to the ground.* So Ezra ascended a platform, and the congregation was before him. He unfolded the Word of God and was about to expound the text. The people stood to their feet, and at that point Ezra began to pray. Verse 6 indicates that he blessed the Lord and praised God, saying, "God, thank you. Thank you for bringing us to this point. Thank you for bringing us back home from our long exile. Thank you for giving us your Word, which we can now study together. Thank you, God, for redeeming us. Thank you for your great plans for us. God, please help us. Have mercy on us. Help us to be pleasing to you." And as he prayed, the entire congregation repeated, "Amen, Amen," which means, "Yes, indeed, God. What Ezra said, we say too. We believe it, too. And we thank you."

The people lifted up their hands, not to have an existential encounter with God or to feel God's presence, as you might find in a modern charismatic service. It was not like that at all. Instead, it was like the posture of a small child reaching for his parents' help. Those of you with small kids, grandkids, or nieces or nephews may have had a similar experience. The little ones come up to your feet and pull themselves up. They look up and reach their hands to you. They want you to bend down, to come down to help them, or maybe they want you to lift them up to you. That was the posture of the Israelite worshipers—hands lifted up as if to say, "God, come down and minister to us by your Spirit. Help us, God." Then Nehemiah writes in Verse 6 that *they bowed low and worshiped Yahweh with their faces to the ground*, another typical posture in worship that involves crouching down to the ground and communicating that God is high and you are low. He is the king; you are the subject.

You see, friends, true worship is never about us. It is not about inspiring us, encouraging us, or meeting our felt needs. We may experience those emotions during our time in worship, but they are not the ultimate aim. Worship aims to give God the praise he deserves—to praise him in word, song, prayer, and obedience. That is what the word "worship" means: to ascribe worth to God, which the Israelites did on this occasion. Every worship service must do the same to glorify God. Now, we come to the final feature of a God-honoring worship service.

VII. God-pleasing corporate worship will be solemn and orderly. Now, friends, as I look at Nehemiah 8:1-8, I cannot help but notice the dramatic difference between Israel's worship and that of the pagan peoples around her. Look at Israel's worship again. All the congregation of Israel—men, women, and children—gathered as one. A worship leader ascended a platform and opened a book. He read from the book and explained its meaning. As he did so, the people responded with obedience and prayer. One man led in prayer, and the others responded with similar words. Together, they lifted their hands and bowed to the ground. The entire service was reverent, orderly, and solemn.

What a far cry from the pagan worship of the day, a good example of which is found in 1 Kings 18. Do you remember when the prophets of Baal tried to worship their false God? Scriptures say that first, they started dancing wildly around their altar. Then they screamed and hollered for hours and hours to get their god's attention, working themselves into an emotional frenzy. Then they hurt themselves, cut themselves with knives, and drew their blood to get their god's attention. Oh, friends, God does not want this from his people. Biblical worship is orderly, targeted at the mind and the will, and dignifies its participants. Only false worship would humiliate its participants or encourage them to lose their minds in the presence of God.

VIII. Conclusion. So, friends, to wrap up today's sermon, here is what God-honoring worship looks like: It is filled with eager participants, led by biblically qualified men, centered on God's Word, aimed at God's glory, and conducted in an orderly fashion. This kind of worship service pleases God. But, oh, how hard it is to maintain. Many pastors are tempted to alter their worship services to make them look and sound more like the world's big gatherings in the vain hope of attracting a larger crowd. And the congregants often cry to have such a worship service. They cry out, "Pastor, give us less thinking and more feeling. Give us less Bible exposition and more skits, plays, and movie clips. Give us fewer organs and more drum sets. Give us less orderliness and more spontaneity." Their cry is always to move worship down the road of worldly entertainment because that type of worship is easier for people. It appeals to their passions, not to their spiritual affections.

So, friends, this morning in the Book of Nehemiah, we see what God-honoring worship looks like but how hard it is to maintain. The only way it will be maintained is if we all work together—the leadership and the congregation—if all of us work together to insist that worship is done God's way, that we submit to his desires for worship, and that we do not ask God to submit himself to our whims. Friends, let us strive for a God-honoring worship service now and always.

CHAPTER TEN

REBUILDING GODLY HOUSEHOLDS

STRONG FAMILIES ARE BUILT ON A SPIRITUAL FOUNDATION AND ARE LED BY GODLY DADS.

I. Introduction to sermon on Nehemiah 8:9-18. Last week, we witnessed Israel's first corporate worship service after Nehemiah's return, and it was a beautiful scene—my favorite in the entire book. The whole congregation of Israel gathered for this event—men, women, and children, about 40,000 people. They stayed together from early morning until midday. As the service began, Ezra, the scribe, ascended a great wooden platform, along with a copy of the Scriptures. The congregation watched as he opened the Scriptures before them. After he opened them, all the people spontaneously rose to their feet. Then, Ezra led the congregation in prayer: "Thank you, God, for bringing us back from our exile, and thank you for helping us rebuild Jerusalem's walls. Thank you for giving us the Scriptures so we might know you and know your will for us." As he prayed, the congregation of Israel replied, "Amen, amen," which meant, "Yes, Lord. We affirm everything that Ezra is saying to you." Ezra then read from the Scriptures while the congregation listened. He expounded God's Word so the people could understand its meaning.

Ezra preached from the platform while the Levites and other religious leaders spread out into this great congregation. They wanted to ensure that everyone could hear and understand the Scriptures, so they repeated Ezra's words to everyone. It was a remarkable event in Israel's history. In Nehemiah 8:8, the prophet wrote that everyone understood the Scriptures due to this service. In today's text, we will see the spiritual impact that God's Word had on this great congregation, especially on their family life. As we work through this passage together, we will learn the following important lesson: Strong families are built on a spiritual foundation and led by godly dads. I want to explore this theme with you today, beginning with the first part of that statement.

II. Strong families are built on a spiritual foundation. Allow me to read Nehemiah 8:9-12 to you: *Then Nehemiah, who was the governor, and Ezra the priest and scribe, and the Levites, who provided the people with understanding, said to all the people, "This day is holy to Yahweh your God; do not mourn or weep." For all the people were weeping when they heard the words of the law. Then he said to them, "Go, eat of the fat, drink of the sweet, and send portions to him who has nothing prepared; for this day is holy to our Lord. Do not be grieved, for the joy of Yahweh is your strength." So the Levites quieted all the people, saying, "Be still, for the day is holy; do not be grieved." Then all the people went away to eat, to drink, to send portions, and to celebrate with great gladness, because they understood the words which had been made known to them.*

These verses give us Israel's reaction to the worship event. We see two major themes arising from them. First is the theme of repentance. As the congregation of Israel listened intently to the Word of God, their collective conscience was pricked because God's Word confronted them with their moral failings. As Ezra read and explained the Scriptures, they understood God's holiness. They understood that God had always been faithful to them, from their nation's founding up to their present time. He was a covenant-keeping God who had fulfilled every last word of his promises. But then they also learned something about themselves: how they were breaking their covenant. They realized that God sent them into exile because they had turned aside to other gods and descended into every form of depravity.

But then they learned how God had regathered them back into the Holy Land again in his grace and in keeping with his promises. As they learned about these two themes, their consciences were struck. They realized their own sinfulness, which caused them to experience genuine repentance. We see the words of repentance throughout this text: mourning, weeping, and grieving. And, friends, all of this was good because repentance is good for the soul. Our *Confession of Faith* explains repentance this way: "Repentance is an evangelical grace," which means genuine repentance is something that God works into our hearts in tandem with his Word. God brings his Word to bear on our lives and awakens us to the reality of our spiritual state before him. He makes us aware of sin and then prompts us to forsake that sin with godly sorrow, to pursue hard after him.

Our *Confession* also states that repentance makes us "sensible of the manifold evils" of our sins. We humble ourselves for them with sorrow, and then we pray for "pardon and strength of grace" so that we can walk before God in a pleasing manner. What we witnessed on that day in Israel was people struck to the very core of their beings by the Word of God, experiencing the godly grief that came when they realized they did not measure up to God's standards. This is why we need regular, sustained exposure to God's Word, which is powerful and sharper than any two-edged sword, piercing even to the division of soul and spirit, joints and marrow. It discerns the thoughts and intentions of our hearts. We need the Word of God to spiritually excavate us, to mine out of us all that is not in line with God's will, to bring it before our eyes so that we can see it, feel sorrow for it, and forsake it, so we can resolve to live a new kind of life.

Friends, spiritual breakthroughs happen this way—through sustained interaction with the Word of God and the Spirit of God working in tandem with his Word to bring conviction and repentance to our hearts. But also understand that God does not want us wallowing in grief either, because doing so would deny his grace. If you were to experience sorrow for any sins that Scriptures reveal to you and then never got beyond the sorrow, if you were to wallow in shame and sadness, that response would suggest that he is not a God of grace who delights to forgive those who repent of their sins and delights to reconcile with people. So, yes, we are called to experience the grief that an awareness of sin brings. However, once we resolve to turn from it and repent, God will have us rejoice in our newfound fellowship with him and rejoice in our pardon. And that response is why we see the second theme in these verses, the theme of rejoicing.

In Nehemiah 8:9-10, the religious leaders told the congregation, *"Do not mourn or weep.... Do not be grieved, for the joy of Yahweh is your strength.* Verse 11 reveals that *the day is holy; do not be grieved."* It was good for the Israelites to feel grief for a moment, but it was not good for the grief to go on without end. It was time for them to turn the page, to go from grief to gladness, because God forgave them. It was time for them to move forward as a new nation. We have an interesting repetition of the words here: "Stop grieving, because this is a holy day." The Levites said a variation of this sentence three times in our text. A holy day should be happy, not sad. It was indeed a sacred day. For the first time in decades, the people gathered as a whole nation to hear the words of the living God. They prayed to God, listened to the Scriptures being read, heard them expounded, and responded to the message with repentance and faith. This event is what holy days are about—dwelling on God's goodness and our relation to him. Yes, grief has a place on a holy day, but that grief should turn quickly to joy, so we find the constant call here: End your suffering. It is time to be happy. Holy days are happy days. Today is the most sacred day we have experienced in a long time. Faith does not require a life of shame, guilt, grief, and fear. It involves a life of basking in God's saving grace in Christ.

In Nehemiah 8:10, Ezra, Nehemiah, and the Levites suggested three ways for the people of Israel to turn their grief into joy on this holy day. The first suggestion was to go back home and feast with their families. They said to the people, "Go your way. The worship event is now over. It is time to go home. Be with your spouses, your kids, and your grandkids." Then Ezra said, *Eat of the fat, drink of the sweet,* which meant, "I want you to go home now and celebrate your forgiveness. Go to your refrigerator [I know they did not have a refrigerator] and pull out your best meat. Feast on it, and take out your sweet wine [which in the ancient Near East was wine mixed with honey, the best wine available]. Take out the sweet wine and enjoy this time with your family. Have a celebration. This is a happy day, not a sad day."

The second part of Verse 10 states, *And send portions to him who has nothing prepared.* Ezra said, "So you and your families make sure that your neighbors have food to celebrate. Do not allow anybody to go without feasting on a happy day like this. Prepare your best food, check on your neighbors, and ensure they have food. If they do not, share what you have with them." And then, finally, Ezra said, "Rejoice in God as a family on this day. Enjoy the culinary riches God has blessed you with and bask in your spiritual riches." These three suggestions are what they told the Israelites to do on this day. Of all the joys in life, there is no greater joy than having a clear conscience before God, to know that nothing is standing between you and your creator. He is yours; you are his. He sees no sin when he looks at you. He sees only you, clothed in the righteousness of his son. To know that all is well between you and your God, that every sin has been washed away, that you have an inheritance waiting for you in heaven, and that you are one of God's saints and one of his holy ones—there is no greater joy!

Charles Spurgeon once said, "Holiness is the royal road to happiness. The death of sin is the life of joy." On this day, Israel's religious leaders declared to the congregation, "You are God's holy people. You have been washed and cleansed, so go home, feast, celebrate, and enjoy the riches God has granted you." We also see here that the key to a happy family life is a family made holy in repentance and faith, a household filled with members who have been convicted by the Word of God, who have expressed their repentance to him, and who can now rejoice together as a redeemed household, just as these households got to enjoy their new spiritual life. Oh, what a joy it is, friends, to be a part of a household where every member—mom, dad, kids, grandkids, extended family, and everyone—knows and loves the Lord. To enjoy that spiritual bond and blood bond between them, there is no greater joy. Strong families are built on a spiritual foundation of repentance, faith, and spiritual rejoicing. However, today's passage also shows that godly parents, especially godly dads, lead strong families.

III. Strong families are led by Godly parents. Let us begin in Verse 13, where Nehemiah writes, *Then on the second day*. So their day of worship was the first day, and Verse 13 addresses the day after that: *on the second day*. Notice that the heads of fathers' houses of all the people, along with the priests and the Levites, came together with Ezra, the scribe, to study the words of the Law. Something special was going on here. Israel had just experienced this incredible worship event where the congregation gathered, heard God's Word, and responded to it. Then they went home, celebrated, and went to bed that night. Now, Verse 13 addresses the next morning. On this new day, we read about all of these dads all over Israel saying, "Was it not amazing yesterday to see God work in the lives of our families? We cannot let this come to an end. We cannot lose the gains that we made yesterday. We must keep up this momentum."

On their own initiative, all of these dads went back the next day to meet with Ezra, Nehemiah, and the religious leaders, saying, "Teach us more. We want to study God's Word under your mentorship. We want everything that you can give us. Then, we will take it back home and share it with our wives and children to keep this spiritual revival going." That response is what we see in this text. Now, friends, I realize we live in a broken world, and in a broken world, many households are without a godly dad. Maybe the dad died in a terrible accident or of a disease, or perhaps the family was torn apart by divorce. Maybe the dad is not a believer. There are many reasons why a home might be without a spiritually active father. In those cases, moms need to take up the mantle of spiritual leadership and ensure that their children are raised in the nurture of the Lord. I thank God for every household with a spiritually vibrant mother who sees that her kids are raised under the Word of God. I thank God for my mom, who took the lead in bringing me and my sister to church every Sunday and making sure that we learned God's ways.

But friends, also understand that the scriptural ideal is to have households with active and godly dads who strive to understand God's Word. On this day in Israel's history, the nation was teeming with godly dads. Verse 13 says they *were gathered to Ezra the scribe that they might gain insight into the words of the law*. The New American Standard Bible says they gathered to *gain insight* into the Scriptures, a good rendering of the Hebrew text. They were coming to gain spiritual wisdom. Ezra gave them more of God's Word and helped them know how it applied to their family life and nation. Having been transformed by God's Word the day before, the Israelite dads were eager to implement all they could of it. Dads, this is your job, and I cannot emphasize enough how important it is.

Yes, you must work hard to put a roof over your family and food on their table. And yes, you should teach your kids how to ride a bike and help them with their homework. They are important, too. But, dads, pay attention to your responsibility to be your home's spiritual leader and take it upon yourself to raise your children in the instruction of the Lord. To be this kind of a dad, you must first be a man of the Word yourself, which means you need to, with God's help, find the motivation to be God's kind of man and to study his Word on your own initiative. And then, out of the overflow of what God is doing in your life, you will raise your children and say, "Kids, this is what God is doing in me. Let me show you how you can live for God, too." A dad who leads his kids in prayer and devotions reads the Scriptures to them and provides sound biblical wisdom when needed. We need these kinds of dads who strive to understand God's Word, bring it back to their families, and make spiritual discoveries from God's Word.

Look at Nehemiah 8:14-15 with me: *They found* [this is all the dads] *written in the law how Yahweh had commanded by the hand of Moses that the sons of Israel should live in booths during the feast of the seventh month, and that they should make the report heard and make a proclamation of it pass throughout all their cities and in Jerusalem, saying, "Go out to the hills, and bring olive branches and wild olive branches, myrtle branches, palm branches, and branches of other leafy trees, to make booths, as it is written."* So, these fathers met with Ezra and other religious leaders to get grounded in the faith. As they studied the Scriptures with Ezra, these dads discovered a festival God prescribed for Israel: the Festival of Booths, sometimes called the Feast of Booths or the Feast of Tabernacles. They were completely ignorant of this festival, but as they dug into God's Word together as dads with good mentors, they rediscovered it. Now, what is a booth? It is a little shelter made of leaves and branches. The Festival of Booths was an annual event prescribed for Israel in the Law of Moses to commemorate Israel's wilderness wanderings. Remember when God rescued the Israelites from Egypt? They spent forty years in the wilderness before entering the Promised Land. During that wilderness wandering, they lived in homemade shelters, tents, and other such housing.

The Festival of Booths commemorated those wanderings. For one week, beginning on the fifteenth day of the seventh month of each year, every Israelite family would give up the comforts of home and live in a homemade booth, just as their ancestors had done. This festival reminded them of how God provided for them throughout their wanderings and was still providing for them. It was meant to inspire their trust in God, knowing that God would always look after them and lead and guide them. On this day, these fathers in Israel discovered the Festival of Booths while studying the Scriptures. Looking at their calendars, they realized they were to celebrate this festival in less than two weeks. From the beginning of Chapter 8, we read that they were already on the second day of the seventh month. The festival was on the fifteenth day of the seventh month, so they had fewer than two weeks to pull this festival off.

So what would they do? The spiritually immature might make excuses and say, "Oh no, a week-long festival. Let us put that on next year's calendar. We will be sure to observe it then. There is no way we can pull this off in thirteen days." That response is what the immature would do. But remember, these dads were on fire. They just attended a grand corporate worship event and thus had a fire lit underneath them. They spent all this time with Ezra, trying to lead their families, and now they had discovered the Festival of Booths. There was no way they would let this slide for a year. So they checked the calendar and said, "Okay, we have fewer than two weeks to pull it off. We had better get to work. Yeah, we just built an entire wall for an entire city and had this massive worship event. But let us go ahead and plan for a giant festival, too." They got right to work and did so promptly with rejoicing and precision.

Look at Verse 16: *So the people went out and brought them and made booths for themselves, each on his roof.* Back then, roofs were flat, which made a good spot for a homemade shelter. Others made booths in their courts, small yards, the temple court, the square at the Water Gate on the city's east side, or the square at the Gate of Ephraim on the west side. All that was required was a nice, ample open space on rooftops, backyards, temple courtyards, and the courtyards around the city's main gates—anywhere they could find an open space. Families all over Jerusalem started to build these small, ramshackle huts in which to live for seven days.

Verse 17 says they did so with great rejoicing: *And there was exceedingly great gladness.* This festival was fun, and the people of Jerusalem were so happy to be rebuilding their national life. In Verse 17, Nehemiah also writes, *The entire assembly of those who had returned from the captivity made booths and lived in the booths.* From the days of Joshua, the son of Nun (and successor to Moses), and from Joshua's time to their time, Israel did not conduct this festival properly. Centuries had passed since it was done correctly. They were excited to follow the Scriptures with a new spiritual life burning inside them. They were fulfilling the terms of their covenant with God, so there was great rejoicing on this day. In Verse 18, Nehemiah writes, *And he [Ezra] read from the book of the law of God daily, from the first day to the last day. And they celebrated the feast seven days, and on the eighth day there was a solemn assembly according to the legal judgment.* So, after the festival was over, it was time for another national worship service, and they held it according to the rules, exactly as the Scriptures prescribed.

My friends, strong nations are built on strong families, and godly dads lead strong families. On this day in Israel's history, the nation was coming back to life because they rebuilt their households on spiritual foundations. And they had dads all over the nation who were taking it upon themselves to learn God's Word, to make discoveries from his Word, to take those discoveries back to their wives, children, and grandchildren, and to implement every last letter of God's Word.

IV. Applications. So, dads, I am going to pick on you this morning. Let me ask you how it is going. What kind of leadership are you providing in your homes? Does your family look to you as the spiritual leader? Are you known for having spiritual gravitas? If not, here is what it will take to become that kind of man. First, regular participation in public worship will be required. I say this because that is how Nehemiah 8 begins. A public worship service lit the fire under these dads so they could return to their homes and become spiritual leaders. So, dads, if you want to be a spiritual leader in your household, you must prioritize public worship.

I may be speaking to the choir, because everyone here is in worship right now. However, I know that over time, the temptation can arise to sleep in, make excuses, and become lax in your commitment to worship. Dads, I cannot envision a scenario where your family will be spiritually better off by your absence from church. I know that times can arise when you need to be away. Some of you are first responders, so you need to staff the hospital every other weekend or make your police rounds. Schedules like that will happen, but we cannot get into a long-term, weekly habit of missing public worship because that is where continuous absences begin. Hearing the Word of God read and sung, prayed and expounded, will do something good inside of you.

I have heard this testimony from more than one man in our church: "You know, Pastor, I was feeling spiritually lethargic, and then I started coming more consistently to worship on Sundays, which has changed my life." I have heard this same message from our dads: "Consistent worship changed my life, and now I am a bold witness at work, and now I am a better dad to my kids." They also testify that Sunday morning worship has a positive impact on them. So, dads, if you want to be a spiritual leader in your home, begin by showing your family that you prioritize worship with your church family.

Dads must also commit deeply to personal Bible study and studying the Word of God under trusted mentors. In today's text, the dads were going to Ezra and the other religious leaders of Israel because they wanted to be well-grounded in the Scriptures and needed spiritual mentors with more knowledge than they had to help guide the process. Friends, we can do that today. You have pastors available who would love to meet with you one-on-one, or you could take advantage of our small group opportunities, including midweek options. Our church has a monthly men's breakfast where we discuss the virtues of biblical manhood. We also have growth group classes where you can be in a small group setting with teaching and a question-and-answer period.

You have many opportunities to go beyond the worship service to get grounded in sound theology and the virtues of manhood. You can download and listen to sound Bible commentaries and sermons throughout the week to take advantage of spiritually mature men and their teaching ministries in many ways, thus getting yourself spiritually grounded. It will take this kind of commitment, dads: a commitment to worship, discipleship, and then leading your families to walk in lockstep with the Scriptures. However, this commitment is not something you can manufacture. It must come from the overflow of God's work in your life. As you come to know and love God more, you will feel your commitment to him grow. As your commitment grows, you will want the people you love to know God, love God, and be committed to him with you. Naturally, it will arise from you, thus prompting you to prioritize Sunday morning, to get your kids discipled in classes and other activities, and to do the work yourself from home. Dads, this is your job. This is the kind of man, the kind of dad, we need you to be.

V. Conclusion. Now more than ever, we need men willing to be spiritual leaders in their homes, like Joshua, who in Joshua 24:15 said to the people of his generation, *"As for me and my house, we will serve Yahweh."* We need men like Ezra and Nehemiah, who are willing to face all kinds of opposition and threats. It meant so much to these two leaders in Jerusalem to lead God's people, and they were willing to endure it all for God's name's sake and their nation's spiritual good. We need men like the dads we witnessed here in Nehemiah 8, who wanted to learn God's Word, take it back to their families, and teach their wives and children. May God give us such godly men.

CHAPTER ELEVEN

REBUILDING OUR RESOLVE PART ONE

REFORMATIONS ARE SUSTAINED AS GOD'S PEOPLE RESOLVE TOGETHER TO BE AS FAITHFUL TO HIM AS HE HAS BEEN TO THEM.

I. Introduction to sermon on Nehemiah 9:1-37. We have discussed reformation extensively in this series on the Book of Nehemiah. Reformation is an intensive effort by God's people to reform their lives and institutions through the Word of God. A related word is revival: a widespread spiritual awakening resulting in new disciples and in re-energized, dispirited disciples. This series has taught us how reformations and revivals are ignited. We have seen that they happen when the Spirit of God moves among his people, who are then consumed with a newfound zeal for God's cause.

This is what happened to Nehemiah and Ezra. God so worked in them that they burned with passion for the truth of God, the people of God, and the cause of God, such that they wanted to lead God's people back to faithfulness, even if it was very costly. This series has also taught us how biblical reformations are fanned into flame by worship. What is worship? It is a special time of interaction between God and his people in which God reveals himself through his Word. Then, his people respond with praise and obedience.

Two weeks ago, we studied the worship service that fueled Israel's ongoing reformation. We saw how the congregation of Israel gathered for this service—more than 40,000 people—men, women, and children. Ezra, the scribe, led the service. We watched him ascend a great wooden platform built for the purpose and take a copy of God's Word. We watched as he opened the Word of God, and the whole congregation spontaneously rose to its feet out of respect for God's Word. Then Ezra read from and expounded the Word. He spoke for hours and hours. As he did so, the people of God lifted their hands in the air, crouched low to the ground, and affirmed the truths of Scripture, along with their commitment to follow God's Word. As a result of that worship service, there was a national moment of repentance, faith, and rejoicing for the pardon received.

Today, friends, we will learn how biblical reformations are sustained over the long haul. Of course, last week, we saw the first part of this sustenance: They were sustained through family worship, which happened after that great worship service. Remember how everyone went home, had their feasts, and slept overnight. Then the following morning, all the dads of Israel said, "We have got to keep the momentum going." So these godly dads got back together with Ezra, the scribe, and said, "Ezra, teach us everything you know. We want it all. We want to return home and immerse our wives and kids in the truths of God's Word." Friends, reformations are sustained in this way: They happen within the household as godly parents commit to instilling God's truths into their children so that what they learn and all their gains can be passed down to the next generation.

Today, we will learn that another way to sustain long-term reformation is when God's people collectively resolve to be faithful to him and make a spiritual resolution to stick closely to God's Word, which is the theme of Nehemiah 9-10. Today, we will examine Chapter 9, where yet another worship service happened. This service occurred just two days after Israel finished celebrating the Festival of Booths. Verses 1-5 give us the details of the service, and Verses 6-37 give us a prayer that Ezra offered during it.

This passage shows us that reformations are sustained when God's people resolve individually and collectively to be as faithful to him as he has been to them. I will say that again. Reformations are sustained as God's people resolve to be as faithful to him as he has been to them. If you want to see a reformation take hold in your day—a reformation of your family life and church, and maybe of society at large—it must begin with you and your heart's commitment. It must start with your resolve before God to be faithful to him, to follow everything you learn in his Word, and to forsake everything that needs to be forsaken. Let us examine Verses 1-5 together to see the necessity of resolving to be faithful.

II. We must resolve together to be faithful to God. As the first part of that resolve, we must repent of every instance of unfaithfulness in our lives. Look at Verse 1 with me, where we see what Israel did in the days of Nehemiah: *Now, on the twenty-fourth day of this month, the sons of Israel gathered with fasting, in sackcloth and with dirt upon them.* So they had an excellent worship service before the festival and then had another one afterward. All of it signifies a service of national repentance. Fasting, sackcloth, and earth on the head are all expressions of repentance. Fasting is when you go without food to express your spiritual needs, as if you are saying, "God, I do not need food right now. What I need is you. I need your grace, your forgiveness, your mercy. I need that more than anything else." So you come to God with hunger pains and then sackcloth (cheap, uncomfortable clothing—think of it like a potato sack—that a repentant person might wear). You wear it to express your spiritual impoverishment before God. Throwing earth on the head was an ancient Near Eastern practice that signified the humility of the repentant person. Overall, they were as low as the ground, which was what they were communicating here. On this day, we see the entire congregation of Israel gathering to express their national repentance once again.

In Verse 2, *The seed of Israel separated themselves from all foreigners.* Understand that this separation was not racial segregation. It was religious segregation. God chose Israel to be a holy nation, to be separated from all of the pagan nations around them. He called them to be a people offering pure worship to him, a people whose lives would model his character and not mirror the character of the unbelievers around them. Pagan nations surrounded Israel. As the exiles returned home, many pagan peoples still lived within the promised land. On this day, to express their spiritual resolve, they came to God fasting, in sackcloth, and with earth on their heads. They came as a separated people, withdrew from all the pagans around them, and wanted to come as a pure, holy, dedicated people to God.

Verse 2 says they stood before God out of respect for him. They came *and confessed their sins and the iniquities of their fathers.* The Scriptures are clear that God does not judge us for the sins of our ancestors. He judges everyone for their own personal sins. However, the sins of a father are often passed down to the son. As you look at your own families, you might say, "My grandfather had a short temper, my father had a short temper, and I have a short temper."

The sins of one generation seem to pass on to the next, which is what Israel was confessing to God on this day: "God, our ancestors were unfaithful to you—our grandfathers and our fathers—and we have been unfaithful in the same way. Forgive us all for our collective sins." This is what repentance looks like. Everything that is unlike God, that does not conform to his will in our lives, must be confessed and forsaken.

Friends, what are you holding on to that you must let go of right now? What sinful habit of life have you gotten yourself trapped in? What decisions are you making? What thought patterns have you cultivated that need to be forsaken? What do you need to talk to God about this very day? Friend, do not delay. Do business with God right here and right now. Do not put it off. If you want reformation to take hold, it must begin with you, with a personal reformation of you resolving to keep short accounts with God. Let go of every sin and then submit to the ministry of God's Word, as we read in Verse 3.

Once we repent of our sins, we must learn to replace those old sinful patterns with new spiritual disciplines, which is what Israel did: Having *confessed their sins and the iniquities of their fathers . . . they rose up in their place and read from the book of the law of Yahweh their God.* So they confessed it all in sackcloth and ashes. They brought themselves joyfully, voluntarily, under the authority of God's Word, saying, "God, we are forsaking everything you disapprove of, and now we want to know what you would have for us." Verse 3 says they did this *for a fourth of the day* or three hours. These people stood on their feet for three hours and listened silently as Ezra expounded upon and read God's Word.

Friends, I am sure these people all had hectic schedules. They had meals to cook, clothes to wash, homes to build, fields to harvest, children to educate, errands to run, and all the rest, just like we do. But none of those tasks kept them from being in God's Word for an extended time. On this day, they understood that hearing from God was the most important thing they could do. I am reminded of the story of Martha and Mary from Luke 10. Do you remember that story? Martha and Mary were sisters, and one day, Jesus came to their house to spend time teaching his disciples. Luke 10 tells us that Martha was running herself ragged the whole time, trying to be the perfect hostess. She was cleaning up, preparing food in the kitchen, and keeping herself busy.

Meanwhile, her sister Mary was sitting at Jesus' feet, soaking in all his teachings. After a while, Martha got frustrated with Mary. She confronted Jesus about it in Luke 10:40, saying, *"Lord, do You not care that my sister has left* me to do all the preparations alone? Then tell her to help me."* In reply, Jesus said in Luke 10:41-42, *"Martha, Martha, you are worried and bothered about so many things, but only one thing is necessary, for Mary has chosen the good part, which shall not be taken away from her."* He emphasized that chores and all the rest were important, but there was also a time for laying all that work aside and tending to the well-being of your soul. That is what the congregation of Israel was doing on this day, and that is what Mary did in her day.

There will be no reformation in our day—not in our lives, churches, community, or society—unless we are willing to step away from the daily tasks of life from time to time to delve into God's Word. We can ignite, fuel, and sustain reformations by the glad submission of God's people to his Word and their response to his Word with a lifestyle of worshipful obedience, which we find from the second part of Verse 3 down to Verse 5. In Verse 3, Nehemiah writes that they re*ad from the book of the law of Yahweh their God for a fourth of the day* and then adds that *for another fourth they were confessing and worshiping Yahweh their God.* So they soaked in God's Word hour after hour and then responded to God's Word with confession. They confessed their faith in God, his worthiness, and their sins. And then they praised God for his work in their lives. Friends, this is what worship is all about. God reveals himself through his Word, and his people respond with praise and obedience. Reformations and revivals are made of this. And it is the most needful thing. If we are to see reformation in our day, we must resolve together to be faithful to God, just as he has been faithful to us.

III. As he has been faithful to us. Verses 6-37 in Chapter 9 record a prayer offered by Ezra, the scribe, during this worship service. The theme of the entire prayer was the faithfulness of God. Before we proceed, here are a few notes about Ezra's prayer. First, as we go through it, notice that the prayer seems to follow the Bible's storyline. It starts with God, moves to creation, and then to the redemption plan. There is a reason for this. For weeks, Israel had been reading God's Word from the very first chapter of the Book of Ezekiel. They were all the way through. As a people, they had been learning the contents of God's Word and the Bible's storyline. So now, as Ezra led the congregation in prayer, he was simply reciting all that they had learned to God, reciting the story of the Bible.

But note something else: The events recounted in this prayer were not just part of Israel's story. They are our story, too, of God's faithfulness to all of us. As the Puritan Matthew Henry said, "God's mercies to our ancestors were mercies to us." We should take all occasions to revive the remembrance of the great things God did for our fathers in olden times. So, friends, realize that as we read the story of God's faithfulness to Israel, we also look at his faithfulness to us because, through Israel, God brought Christ into the world. It is by Christ that we are saved. It is our story, too, so let us work through this prayer together.

We begin with the first part of Verse 6, where Ezra affirms God's uniqueness. He begins, *You alone are Yahweh*. Notice how, in some translations, the word LORD is in all caps because it translates the Hebrew word, Yahweh, the Bible's most precious name for God. It is the name that God revealed to Moses at the burning bush. It means "I am" and speaks to God's infinite nature. He is the God who has always existed and who always will exist. He is not a God who passes through moments of time. He dwells in the eternal present. Yahweh describes God's independence. He does not need creation; creation needs him. It speaks to his self-sufficiency and shows that he is all-knowing, all-present, and all-powerful. He is the one true and living God. "Yahweh" also emphasizes God as a covenant maker and covenant keeper. He revealed this name to Moses when he established a relationship with him. He is a gracious God who reveals himself to people, making them his special people. He works in and through them and does good things for them. He is the God that we worship. He is a God who created all things and upholds all things.

Look at the second part of Verse 6: *You have made the heavens, The heaven of heavens with all their host, The earth and all that is on it, The seas and all that is in them. You give life to all of them, And the heavenly host bows down to You.* This verse echoes Genesis 1. God is the creator. He created all the heavens, the earth, the land, the sea, the vegetation, and all animal life. He preserved it all by his power. The Apostle Paul also echoed these words in Colossians 1:16-17, where he wrote, *For in Him all things were created, both in the heavens and on earth, visible and invisible, whether thrones or dominions or rulers or authorities—all things have been created through Him and for Him. And He is before all things, And in Him all things hold together.*

God is not just the maker; He is that unseen power who holds the universe together, who maintains the laws of nature so this universe does not fly apart. Understand that if God withdrew his presence from us for even one nanosecond, every particle of the universe would break up. All of this shows God's faithfulness to us: moment by moment, day by day, even though we have sinned greatly, he still holds his universe together. He allows your heart to beat another time and gives you another opportunity to suck oxygen into your lungs. All of it is by his faithfulness and grace. And now from creation, as he returns to the story of redemption, beginning with God's calling of Abraham in Verses 7-8, Nehemiah writes, *You are Yahweh God, Who chose Abram And brought him out from Ur of the Chaldees, And gave him the name Abraham. You found his heart faithful before You, And cut a covenant with him To give him the land of the Canaanite, Of the Hittite and the Amorite, Of the Perizzite, the Jebusite, and the Girgashite—to give it to his seed. And You established Your promise, For You are righteous.*

Friends, in the generations following the great flood, humanity continued on its downward trajectory into depravity. It reached a point where the knowledge of the living God had almost vanished from the earth. But at just that moment, God singled out one man from all the races of men—Abram, a worshiper of idols in a pagan land called Ur. God made himself known to Abram and made some remarkable promises to him: "If you follow me to a new land that I will show you, forsaking everything—your false gods, everything you have ever known—I will make you a great nation. And one day, every nation will be blessed through your line." It was a promise that Christ would come through his line. The Scriptures say that Abraham believed God, and God counted it to him for righteousness. He was justified by faith and followed God exactly where God had told him to go. God changed his name from Abram to Abraham, signifying the new relationship. The name "Abram" means "father," and "Abraham" means "father of nations."

This event is the beginning of the story of redemption. God chose Abraham, the forefather of us all. He did not just keep his promises to Abraham, but he also kept them to Abraham's descendants. In Verses 9-15, Ezra prays: *"You saw the affliction of our fathers in Egypt, And heard their cry by the Red Sea. Then You performed signs and wonders against Pharaoh, Against all his servants and all the people of his land; For You knew that they acted presumptuously toward them, And made a name for Yourself as it is this day. You split the sea before them, So they passed through the midst of the sea on dry land; And their pursuers You cast into the depths, Like a stone into mighty waters. And with a pillar of cloud, You led them by day, And with a pillar of fire by night To light for them the way In which they were to go. Then You came down on Mount Sinai, And spoke with them from heaven; You gave them upright judgments and true laws, Good statutes and commandments."* [You are thinking of the Ten Commandments and other statutes.] *So You made known to them Your holy sabbath, And commanded to them commandments, statutes and law, By the hand of Your servant Moses. You gave bread from heaven for them for their hunger, You brought forth water from a rock for them for their thirst, And You said to them to enter in order to possess The land which You swore to give them."*

A few generations after God chose Abraham and settled him in the promised land, a famine broke out. This famine prompted the descendants of Abraham to leave their promised land and go to Egypt, which was a land of plenty. Abraham's descendants made a new home for themselves and prospered there in Egypt for a time. They were wealthy, their children multiplied, and they thrived. However, as time passed and the Israelites' numbers grew, the pharaohs became increasingly uneasy with this massive group of non-native people in their kingdom. Hence, the pharaohs began curtailing the Israelites' liberties. Finally, the descendants of Abraham, the Jewish people, were condemned to chattel slavery in Egypt.

But then they cried out to God for mercy, and God answered them. He raised up the prophet Moses, who led the Israelites out of their enslavement in Egypt and took them back to the promised land, back to the land of Abraham. God did this by unleashing plagues on Egypt and by parting the Red Sea so the Jews could travel through on dry ground and escape their would-be captors. As the Jewish people wandered in the wilderness for forty years, God provided them with food from heaven and water from rocks. He preserved their shoes and clothing until they reached the end of their journey. God did all this because he is a faithful God who works wonders and miracles for his people.

The Old Testament Scriptures contain about 500 references to God as a worker of miracles. Fully half of those references relate to the rescue of the Jews from Egypt. It was a huge event in redemptive history. God also kept his word to the Israelites even when they showed contempt for him, which we read about in Nehemiah 9:16-21. Look at Verse 16 with me: *"But they, our fathers, acted presumptuously; They became stiff-necked and would not listen to Your commandments."* Do you see the contrast here? God was faithful to them, but they were not reciprocating with him. The phrase "stiffened their neck" conveys the image of a pair of oxen wearing a yoke. Understand that the farmer does not place the yoke on the neck of his oxen to punish them. He does it to guide the oxen to walk in straight paths so he can plant and harvest.

In the same way, God gathered the descendants of Abraham, forged them into a nation, and gave them his Ten Commandments and many other statutes. These commandments and statutes were not punishments for the people of God. They existed to guide them in straight paths and show them how they should go. Sometimes, oxen are stubborn and do not accept the yoke a farmer places on their necks. They will stiffen their necks and veer to the right or the left. They will refuse the farmer's direction. In the same way, the long history of Israel tells the story of a people who stiffened their necks against

God, who would not walk the straight paths that God laid out for them, but who turned aside to the right and the left, worshiped false gods, embraced every abomination, and degraded themselves in the process. But even so, God was faithful.

Nehemiah writes in Verse 17, *"But You are a God of lavish forgiveness, Gracious and compassionate, Slow to anger and abounding in lovingkindness; And You did not forsake them."* In Verse 19, he writes, *"But You, in Your abundant compassion, Did not forsake them in the wilderness."* And then, in Verses 20-21, he writes, *"You gave Your good Spirit to give them insight, Your manna You did not withhold from their mouth, And You gave them water for their thirst. Indeed, forty years You sustained them in the wilderness, and they did not lack; Their clothes did not wear out, nor did their feet swell."* God kept his word in all of Israel's history. Every act of judgment and deliverance was precisely according to his Word.

Verses 26-31 record the times of the judges and the kings of Israel, times in which Israel was constantly going astray, making a mess of their lives, and then crying out to God for help again. What did God do? Every last time, he came when they called. He rescued them from the hands of their enemies and rebuilt them. Even then, the people of Israel were witnessing God's faithfulness, allowing their return to the Promised Land after being taken into captivity by first the Assyrian empire, then the Babylonians, and then the Persians. God was bringing them back and allowing them to rebuild the walls of Jerusalem. He was reconstituting this nation again.

God is always faithful to his people, so in Verses 32-37, the people of Israel, through their great scribe, Ezra, came to their creator again in repentance. They knew if they did, God would restore them. In 2 Chronicles 7:14, God made this promise to Israel: If *My people who are called by My name humble themselves and pray and seek My face and turn from their evil ways, then I will listen from heaven, I will forgive their sin, and I will heal their land.* They prayed to God because they knew he would listen, forgive, and restore them again. They knew their national reformation could continue. God says much the same to us today. The Apostle John in 1 John 1:8-9 writes, *If we say that we have no sin, we deceive ourselves, and the truth is not in us. If we confess our sins, He is faithful and righteous to forgive us our sins and to cleanse us from all unrighteousness.*

IV. Application and Conclusion. My friends, we are living in difficult times today. We are witnessing tyranny rise all over the world and seeing difficult days for the Church of Christ in many places. Here in the States, we are watching the Church's numbers decline and her courage fail. It seems like this trajectory will continue until the situation worsens. However, it does not need to be that way. God can do another work among us. He brought the Great Awakening in colonial times and can give us another today if he chooses. He led a great reformation in Europe in the 16th century and can bring reformation to us, too. There is no reason why this trajectory must continue on a downward slope forever. But friends, if there is to be a revival or a reformation, it must begin with us. It must start with our willingness to repent of every sin, come under the authority of God's Word, and say, "Whatever God says, I will do." We must also be willing to bear Christ's yoke and to walk in his straight paths. Christ said in Matthew 11:30, *"For my yoke is easy and My burden is light."* There is no hardship to walk in the way of Christ.

Once again, if there is to be a reformation or a revival, it must begin with each of us. And then perhaps God will use us to reach others and do a great work. Maybe you are thinking, "Pastor, you do not know what I have done." That is true, but God knows, and if God can reconcile with Israel after all she did, then I know he will reconcile with you no matter what you have done. Or maybe you are thinking, "Pastor, it is too late for me. I have been in a pattern of sin for too long. Too many bad consequences have mounted—as many bad consequences as Israel experienced." Have you been in a pattern of sin as long as Israel was? Oh, friends, if God can reconcile with her, he can reconcile with you. Or maybe you are saying, "I do not even know where to begin." Well, begin with confession. Confess everything to God: Confess your faith, confess your sins, and plead for him to restore you. My friends, reformations are sustained when God's people resolve to be as faithful to him as he has been to them. It begins with repentance and remembering God's faithfulness.

Chapter Twelve

REBUILDING OUR RESOLVE PART TWO

Spiritual resolutions are expressed through repentance and rededication.

I. Introduction to sermon on Nehemiah 9:38–10:39. Last week, I started the sermon by discussing the nature of reformations. I would like to begin there again this week, starting with a definition. A reformation is an intensive effort by God's people to reform their lives and institutions through the Word of God. The Book of Nehemiah is about reformation and shows how they are ignited. It happens when the Spirit of God moves among his people, and they become zealous for his cause. They become willing to say whatever needs to be said, do whatever needs to be done, and see their lives and churches reformed by the Word of God, regardless of the personal cost.

Nehemiah also shows us how reformations are fueled. It happens through worship. What is worship? It is a special time of interaction between God and his people in which God reveals himself to them through the Word, and they respond to him through praise and obedience. Several weeks ago, we studied the worship service that fueled Israel's ongoing reformation in Nehemiah's day. The entire congregation of Israel gathered for that worship service, about 40,000 men, women, and children. Ezra, the scribe, led this worship service. He ascended a great wooden platform built for the purpose, took a copy of God's Word, and opened the Scriptures before the people, who spontaneously rose to their feet. Ezra then prayed to the congregation and thanked God for every instance of his grace to Israel. The people responded by saying, "Amen, Amen," which meant, "Yes, God, we affirm everything Ezra says, too." Then Ezra read from and expounded upon God's Word for hours and hours. God's people in Israel listened, repented of their sins, and trusted in God's promises. A great national reformation began to take shape. Friends, that is what reformations are made of: When God's people gather and bring themselves under the authority of his Word, they repent, express their faith through worship, and praise God for all he does. This is a reformation.

The Book of Nehemiah also shows us how the gains made during a reformation can be sustained over the long haul. The first way is through family discipleship, especially when Christian dads take it upon themselves to be the spiritual leaders of their homes, commit to learning all they can from God's Word, and then impart that knowledge to their wives and children. It happens when moms and dads commit to sharing the riches of the faith with their kids. In this way, the reformations gained in one generation are passed on to the next. There is another way that spiritual reforms can be sustained in the long term. We will see that today. It happens when God's people pledge to be as faithful to him as he has been to them and hold themselves accountable for maintaining that pledge.

II. We must hold ourselves accountable for keeping our spiritual resolutions. This step is critical to sustaining a reformation. If you want a reformation to take hold in your own day, it must begin here—with you and with us as a congregation. We must resolve to be faithful to God in every way, listen to his Word, implement his Word in every department of our lives and church, hold ourselves accountable before God, and be accountable to each other to maintain our commitment. We see those resolves in today's text.

Let us pick it up now in Nehemiah 9:38. We will start here because, in the Hebrew Bible, this verse begins Chapter 10, which says, *"Now because of all this We are cutting an agreement in writing; And on the sealed document are the names of our princes, our Levites, and our priests."* Friends, Israel made remarkable progress throughout this book. As we have studied it together, we have seen the Jewish exiles return to the Holy Land, rebuild the walls of their capital city, Jerusalem, and engage in these seasons of national repentance. We have seen them reinstitute corporate worship and have thus seen great things emerge. We have seen them revive their historic festivals and holy days and rebuild their family discipleship. The nation has undergone a tremendous reformation. Yet, the Book of Nehemiah is also sensitive to Israel's history. The nation's people knew that for many generations, they had been unfaithful to God and their covenant with God, and they knew it could happen again. So, to hold on to their gains and keep this reformation alive from generation to generation, they decided to get together and ratify a new national covenant. Even better, they determined to reaffirm their old covenant, which God had made with them at Mount Sinai generations earlier. This renewed covenant had four essential features. We see them here in Verse 38.

First, they said it would be an agreement or a firm covenant. This agreement could also be translated as a binding covenant. It would be a legal document that would include tangible blessings for maintaining their commitments but real consequences for breaking them. They put teeth to their verbal commitments, saying, "Look, we want this reformation to hold. We do not want our nation to backslide as it has in the past, so we will stand before God, make new vows to him, and reaffirm our commitment. We are putting teeth into this one. It will be a binding agreement between us and God."

Secondly, they put it in writing, which spoke to the seriousness of their commitment, because it would be in the form of a public document visible to everyone, believer and non-believer, Jew and pagan, God and man. Everyone would see this document; therefore, the people of God would be held to their commitments. It would also be a sealed document, which we find in Verse 38. In those days, sealing a document marked your official consent to its terms. It made the legal document official. They also signed their names on the document, which we read in Nehemiah 10:1-27. By my count, there were 84 names here. Nehemiah's name was at the top because he was the governor of Israel. Following his name were the names of other political leaders, Levites, and priests. And friends, these 84 names represented the entire congregation of Israel of the day. Look at 10:28-29 with me: *Now the rest of the people—the priests, the Levites, the gatekeepers, the singers, the temple servants, and all those who had separated themselves from the peoples of the lands to the law of God, their wives, their sons and their daughters—all those who had knowledge and understanding, are joining with their relatives, their nobles, and are entering into a curse and an oath to walk in God's law.* So, we have 84 signatories to the document, but they represented everyone—men, women, children, all the people of Israel. They were all going to hold themselves to this new covenant.

We see something remarkable happening in ancient Israel here—a people who, for so many generations, had been unfaithful to God, had turned to worship idols, had plunged into every form of moral depravity, had never kept their promises to God, and had suffered the devastating consequences of it. They were thrown into exile and forced to live in foreign lands, but now, by the grace of God, they were able to return to their homeland. Slowly but surely, these caravans of exiles returned to the promised land, and this time, they wanted things to be different. So, a reformation was sparked in this nation. They rebuilt their city's walls, they reinstituted their worship, they repented of their sins, and fathers got serious about discipling their kids. All was going well, and then came the grand climax of this national reawakening: They wrote a covenant that reaffirmed the original one. They sealed it, put their names to it, and promised to hold themselves accountable to keep its terms.

Of course, you and I understand that we are not a part of national Israel because we have no part in her national covenants. We are a "new covenant" people who belong to Christ's Church. Yet, there is much for us to learn from Israel's actions on this day. I believe the chief lesson here is about God being merciful and gracious, eager to forgive his people and reconcile when they come to him in repentance and faith. I say this because that is why Israel wrote their new covenant document. They understood that they had been unfaithful to God for many generations and had done unspeakable deeds. They knew how awful their history as a nation had been. Yet, they also knew who their God was: a loving, gracious, and merciful God. They knew the promise he made to them earlier, that if his people, who are called by his name, would humble themselves, repent of their sins, and seek his face anew, he would receive them. He would forgive their sins and heal their land. They knew these promises. That is why they came to God as a great congregation on this day. They drew up a new covenant and signed their names to it. They understood that if they did this, God would receive them again.

Friends, there is a lesson about God in these verses. It does not matter who you are, what you have done, or how long you have been away from him. It matters not because the God of heaven is a God of grace, and he will receive you no matter what. All you need to do is approach him in humility, repent of your sins, trust in him, and cling to the all-sufficiency of his atonement through Jesus Christ. That is all you have to do, and he will receive you as his child. Or if you are his child already but have backslidden, he will renew his fellowship with you. That is the kind of God he is.

There is another important lesson in these verses regarding repentance and what true repentance looks like. True repentance is rooted in the will, not the emotions. It is rooted in the will, not the feelings. Here is what I mean: Repentance can include godly grief and even weeping over one's sins, but it does not stop there. Repentance is more than just feeling your conscience pricked by the sins you have committed. It is more than just weeping over the bad consequences you have experienced because of sinful choices. True repentance occurs when you, deep in your soul and will, experience a change in your heart. You no longer desire a life away from God and no longer want to practice those old sins. Instead, your desire is now for God. You now see the beauty of his holiness, the loveliness of his Law, and the urge to follow hard after God. That is repentance. Yes, you may weep because the life that was wasted in those sins has grieved you, but now you are determined to follow after God.

Friends, that is repentance: a movement of the will. This new covenant document that Israel signed on this day was simply the fruit of their genuine repentance. They made a decisive break with their sins and said, "We do not want to be away from God anymore. We want him now. We want the joy of his presence in our lives." So they wrote this document, which was the fruit of their repentance, and said, "We are going to follow God now." This is what true repentance looks like. Their example is how you know whether you truly mean to do business with God and what you are doing about your sins. Have you continued to sin despite the emotional pain it brings you, or have you made a decisive break? Have you declared that a change needs to happen? Has there been a movement of your will away from all of that and toward God through Christ? That is repentance.

A third important lesson from these verses concerns the importance of accountability structures to help us maintain a godly walk. The Israelites' covenant document was exactly that—an accountability tool. They were making a legal document that was public, signed, and sealed. They held each other accountable and invited God to hold them to it, bless them as they kept it, and curse them if they rejected it. Friends, we must maintain healthy accountability structures as a local church and individual Christian disciples.

These structures are part of what it means to join a local church. When you come to faith in the Lord Jesus Christ, you first present yourself to a local church. You offer a testimony of conversion, and then the congregation baptizes you in the name of the triune God, which signifies a break from your old life. At that point, you are being raised to a new life in Christ. Then, as you join that local church, you sign your name. At our church, you sign your name on a paper that declares, "I affirm my faith in the Lord Jesus Christ. I affirm my desire to maintain a Christian walk. I am asking all of you to hold me accountable. I will help you be accountable for it." Everyone signs a church covenant when they join and holds one another accountable. We do not see this process as a burden but as a good and necessary step, a tool to help us persevere long-term so that we never walk away from the Lord.

Accountability structures are good for us and for individual Christians, too. Perhaps you are a church member already, but maybe you have one particular vice—what we sometimes call a besetting sin—that you have tried to overcome repeatedly but cannot gain victory over. It may be time to take this issue to the next step and bring other believers in. Stop trying to overcome it alone. Bring one or two Christian brothers and sisters around you to help establish an accountability partnership. Invite them to ask you regularly how this battle against your sin is going. Invite them to read the Scriptures with you and meditate on their teachings together. Invite others into your life to hold you accountable. This humble step is often necessary for overcoming deeply rooted vices.

Friends, this passage shows us how important accountability can be for maintaining a long-term godly walk. But then, as we do this together, it is also good for us to be very specific about the new path we want to follow. We must break away from our old ways of living and lay out a concrete course going forward. This accountability structure is what we find here in Nehemiah 10:28-39, and we have details about their covenant commitments.

III. We must be clear about the commitments we are resolving to keep.
The Israelites started with the general and then moved to the specific. Let us start with their general commitment in 10:28-29, where Nehemiah writes, *Now the rest of the people—the priests, the Levites, the gatekeepers, the singers, the temple servants, and all those who had separated themselves from the peoples of the lands to the law of God, their wives, their sons and their daughters—all those who had knowledge and understanding, are joining with their relatives, their nobles, and are entering into a curse and an oath to walk in God's law, which was given by the hand of Moses, God's servant, and to keep and to do all the commandments of Yahweh our Lord and His judgments and His statutes.* These verses describe their covenant renewal: a renewed commitment to walk in the Law of God.

Immediately after rescuing the Israelites from their enslavement in Egypt, God met with the Jewish people at Mount Sinai. There, he took a ragtag group of formerly enslaved people, constituted them as a nation, and gave them their national constitution—the Ten Commandments, ten laws from God written on stone tablets. In addition to the Ten Commandments, God gave them many other statutes and ordinances, fleshing out the Ten

Commandments into all of life's departments. These holy laws were good laws that would lead to flourishing if the nation observed them, but for many years, the Israelites forsook them. They chased after other gods, sacrificed their own offspring to these false gods, and plunged themselves into every form of immorality. They destroyed their nation in the process, so on this day, they renewed their commitment by saying, "We will walk by God's good law from now on—no more backsliding. No more turning away from God. We are going to keep it."

In Verses 30-37, the Israelites got very specific by outlining how their ancestors had failed God. They asserted their determination to be different and walk in God's ways. First, we see their commitment in Verse 30 to reject every form of syncretism, which involves the mixing of true religion with false religion, *and that we will not give our daughters to the peoples of the land or take their daughters for our sons.* In the past, the sons and daughters of Israel gave themselves in marriage to the pagan peoples around them, and the result was not that those pagan peoples converted to Judaism. Instead, those Jews converted to paganism. These conversions were never a racial matter. They were a religious matter. By marrying the pagan peoples around them, they became like the pagans themselves. They did not want this to happen again and were determined that, this time, they would follow God's law by marrying within the faith. This way, God would perpetuate their nation and faith to the next generation. They were not going to fall into syncretism again.

In Verse 31, the Israelites renewed their commitment to keep the Sabbath laws: *As for the peoples of the land* [this statement refers to the pagans who live in and about Israel] *who bring wares or any grain on the sabbath day to sell, we will not receive from them on the sabbath or a holy day; and we will forego the crops the seventh year and the exaction of every debt.* The fourth commandment says to remember the Sabbath day and keep it holy. God had prescribed for Israel that on one day of every week, each Saturday, they were to lay aside their regular labors and spend the day resting and worshiping God. The Jewish people never followed that law. They had other Sabbath laws, including one that said the Jews must allow their land to rest every seventh year. They could not grow crops year after year in perpetuity—doing so would destroy the ground. Every seventh year, the land needed to rest and rebuild its nutrients, and then it could be planted the following year. They never kept that law either. Greed prevented them from taking a year off from their planting and harvesting. They never obeyed the Sabbath laws, but now that their nation was experiencing a reformation, they were determined to keep those Sabbath laws. Every Saturday, they committed to lay aside their labors, to rest, and then to worship God because they understood that worship is the fuel that sustains a reformation. If you neglected worship, every other aspect of life would fall apart. Worship kept it all together, so they prioritized their day of worship, and every seventh year, they would give their land the required rest. From this point forward, they would follow God's law.

Then, in Verses 32-37, we see a renewal of their commitment to support the Lord's work. In Verses 32-33, they promised to support it with monetary donations. They also promised to donate their time and energy to the Lord's work in Verse 34: *Likewise, we cast lots for the supply of wood among the priests, the Levites, and the people, in order to bring it to the house of our God, according to our fathers' households, at fixed times annually, to burn on the altar of Yahweh our God, as it is written in the law.* The Law stated that the Temple's fire on the altar must always be an eternal flame. Of course, this required a lot of wood and a constant supply. On this day, the Israelites divided into families and cast lots. Each family would take one day of the year when it would bring a supply of wood to keep the fire on the altar burning. They committed their money, their time, and their resources. In Verses 35-37, we see their promise to donate property to the Lord's cause. They pledged to give the Lord the first fruits of their crops, livestock, wine, and oil. Everything they had, the first and the best of all, was going to the temple service because worship was the most important thing.

In Verse 36, the Israelites even pledged their firstborn sons. Look at that verse with me, starting with Verse 35: *and to bring the first fruits of our ground and the first fruits of all the fruit of every tree to the house of Yahweh annually, and to bring to the house of our God the firstborn of our sons and of our cattle, and the firstborn of our herds and our flocks as it is written in the law, for the priests who are ministering in the house of our God.* They pledged their firstborn sons, not to be sacrificed but to dedicate them to the Lord's work. Understand what a tremendous sacrifice this would have been. If they dedicated their firstborn son to temple service, they could not use him to help plant and harvest crops, maintain their homestead, or watch their livestock. It would have been an economic hardship for the family. But again, worship was the most important thing. To ensure that God's worship was sustained generation after generation, every family promised on this day that they would disciple their children so that they would desire to serve God more than anything else. They also promised to offer their firstborn sons to the Temple, to God, to give themselves as temple servants, gatekeepers, and laborers for the sake of God. They were ready to give everything to God.

Finally, in Verses 38-39, they pledged to be faithful stewards of everything donated to the Lord's work: *And the priest, the son of Aaron, shall be with the Levites when the Levites receive tithes, and the Levites shall bring up the tenth of the tithes to the house of our God, to the chambers of the storehouse. For the sons of Israel and the sons of Levi shall bring the contribution of the grain, the new wine and the oil to the chambers; the utensils of the sanctuary are there, as well as the priests who are ministering and the gatekeepers and the singers. Thus, we will not forsake the house of our God.* What we have here is the setup of a system of checks and balances. We see a chain of custody established for the handling of all donations to the Temple because they wanted to be sure that every last item donated to the Lord's work would go to the Lord's work, that not one penny of it, not even one glass of wine, would be misused.

Now, friends, it is clear from this passage that these people followed God's Word seriously. They rejected syncretism, kept the Sabbath laws, supported the Lord's work as their primary focus, maintained their worship, and discipled their children in God's ways to ensure that the gains made during this precious time in their history would not be lost.

IV. Conclusion. As we begin this new year together, we will all do well to remember our commitments to God and one another as fellow church members. We should renew our commitments to one another, so I have included our church covenant in today's bulletin. Everyone who joins our congregation signs a document saying, "I have read the church covenant. I affirm everything it says and will keep these promises. These are my promises to my new church family. I will maintain them." It also asks the congregation to keep us faithful. When I sign, I am asking you to hold me accountable for these promises. When you sign, you are asking me to hold you to it.

Friends, this is a great way to start our new year together and pull out that old church covenant. Maybe you last saw it the day you joined. Let us read it together and renew our promises as a church family. May God use this to instill in us a longing to be faithful to God's Word and reform our lives and church according to his standards. May God use our commitment to do great things in our city and beyond this new year. I will read the plain text; we will all read the bold.

"Having been led as we believe by the Spirit of God, to receive the Lord Jesus Christ as our Savior, and on the profession of our faith, having been baptized in the name of the Father, and of the Son, and of the Holy Spirit, we do now in the presence of God, angels, and this assembly, most solemnly and joyfully enter into covenant with one another, as one body in Christ.

"We engage, therefore, by the aid of the Holy Spirit, to walk together in Christian love; to strive for the advancement of this church in knowledge and holiness; to promote its prosperity and spirituality; to sustain its worship, ordinances, discipline, and doctrines; to contribute cheerfully and regularly to the support of the church, the relief of the poor, and the spread of the gospel through all nations.

"We also engage to educate our children in the Christian faith; to seek the salvation of our kindred and acquaintances; to walk circumspectly in the world; to be just in our dealings, faithful in our engagements, and exemplary in our deportment; to avoid all gossip, backbiting, and unrighteous anger.

"We further engage to watch over one another in brotherly love; to remember each other in prayer; to aid each other in sickness and distress; to cultivate Christian sympathy in feeling and courtesy in speech; to be slow to take offense, but always ready for reconciliation and mindful of the rules of our Savior to secure it without delay.

"We, moreover, engage that when we move from this place, we will as soon as possible unite with another church, where we can carry out the spirit of this covenant and the principles of God's Word." Amen.

Chapter Thirteen

Rebuilding with Godly Leadership

To lead well, you must know the qualities of godly leadership.

I. Introduction to sermon on Nehemiah 11:1–12:47. It is no secret that the American Church is facing a leadership crisis today. Part of the problem is that fewer leaders are coming through the pipeline. Many American churches are without a pastor and have no prospects of one anytime soon. However, another side of the problem is that many pastoral leaders are simply unqualified for the work. Churches are so desperate to fill their pulpits that they have abandoned the entire vetting process.

For example, in just two weeks, a lead pastor in Fort Lauderdale, Florida, was forced to resign following allegations of bullying and financial mismanagement. A senior teaching pastor in Fort Worth, Texas, resigned after being charged with unlawfully carrying a weapon and driving under the influence with a minor. A pastor from Chickasha, Oklahoma, was jailed after being charged with three counts of indecent conduct with a minor. A lead student pastor in Phoenix, Arizona, was fired for having an affair with a church employee. On and on it goes—these examples occurred in just two weeks. So, I say again, there is a serious leadership crisis in the American Church today.

The Church needs to relearn what genuine godly leadership looks like and insist that her leaders model godly behavior. These needs are why we need the Book of Nehemiah so badly today. You see, the book is a master class in godly leadership. It follows Nehemiah's career from the moment he accepted the mantle of leadership in Israel through the leadership he exercised in Israel as he sought to rebuild and revitalize God's chosen nation. It shows us what godly leadership looks like and how godly leaders inspire God's people to do God's work in God's way.

Friends, I want to work through this passage with you today and draw attention to its leadership principles. We are in Nehemiah 11-12, a large passage of Scripture for me to preach on in one morning. In these chapters, Nehemiah's leadership abilities come to the forefront. We will see five leadership qualities we must learn to practice as a local church. I want to discuss these five qualities so we can always make good leadership decisions as a church. Let us go through them together now.

II. Godly leaders lead by example. Look at the first part of Nehemiah 11:1 with me: *And the officials of the people lived in Jerusalem*, which refers to Nehemiah, Ezra, and a few other key players. We have learned a lot of important information about Jerusalem through this series. It was the most important city in ancient Israel and the focus of Nehemiah's rebuilding efforts. However, we have also learned that it was a dangerous city because none of the nations around Israel wanted to see Jerusalem rebuilt. They saw a rebuilt Jerusalem as a threat to their national security, so guys like Sanballat, Tobiah, Geshem, and many other foreign leaders constantly tried to get Nehemiah and the workers to stop their rebuilding.

They mocked and threatened Nehemiah and the workers. They raised up troops to invade Jerusalem to try and take out the city. Even after its walls were rebuilt, Jerusalem remained vulnerable because, according to Nehemiah 7:4, *the city was large and spacious, but the people in it were few*. There were not enough able-bodied men to adequately defend it. Yet, Nehemiah, Ezra, and the other key leaders of Israel chose to live there because they believed in Israel's revitalization and that a vibrant capital city was the key to rebuilding it. Despite its dangers, these men had no problem being the first to live there. They hoped their courageous presence would inspire other Israelites to join them so Jerusalem could finally be secured. This is leadership: True leaders lead by example.

If you want your people to be courageous, you must be courageous. If you want them to be faithful, you must be faithful. If you want your people to make sacrifices for the cause, you must make sacrifices for the cause. You must be the first to act, and your courage and sacrifices must be the greatest. You must model in your own life the virtues that you want to see in the people you are leading. Friends, this is what leadership is all about.

You may have seen the old war movie *We Were Soldiers*, starring Mel Gibson as Lieutenant Colonel Hal Moore, depicting the first major Vietnam War battle. Colonel Moore was sent to North Vietnam with 400 soldiers to fight in the first battle. When he landed, he learned what his mission would be: He and his 400 soldiers would have to eliminate a North Vietnamese force that had just recently attacked an American base. The trouble was that American intelligence had no idea how many North Vietnamese soldiers were involved in that attack, so the battle commenced with Moore and his men, who were completely blind to what they were up against.

Early in the battle, they captured a North Vietnamese scout and learned that they would be up against 4,000 North Vietnamese troops: 400 Americans versus 4,000 North Vietnamese. The movie followed Colonel Moore as he prepared his troops for this great battle and tried to bolster their courage to face their foes. In the film's most famous speech, which reflected what Colonel Moore told his troops, he said, "I can't promise you that I will bring you all home alive. But this I swear, before you and before Almighty God, that when we go into battle, I will be the first to set foot on the field, and I will be the last to step off, and I will leave no one behind. Dead or alive, we will all come home together. So help me, God."

Friends, that speech was leadership by example. Colonel Moore kept his promise, and the movie carefully demonstrated it. They showed his boots being the first to land on the battlefield and the last to leave. He did not step off the battlefield until every one of his soldiers, living and dead, was helicoptered out before him. At one point in the battle, Colonel Moore was told to leave the field to brief his commanding officers on the fight's progress. Hal Moore refused the order and said, "I am not leaving this battlefield while my men are in the thick of it. I am staying with my troops, and they can find out how the battle went after it is done." Friends, if God calls you to be a leader, he is summoning you to model the virtues you want to see in your followers.

As the Apostle Paul said to his young protege, Timothy, in 1 Timothy 4:12-16, *Let no one look down on your youthfulness, but show yourself as a model to those who believe in word, conduct, love, faith, and purity. Until I come, give attention to the public reading of Scripture, to exhortation and teaching. Do not neglect the gift within you, which was given to you through prophetic utterance with the laying on of hands by the council of elders. Take pains with these things; be absorbed in them so that your progress will be evident to all. Pay close attention to yourself and to your teaching; persevere in these things, for as you do this you will save both yourself and those who hear you.* Paul told Timothy, a young church pastor in Ephesus, "Timothy, this must be the focus of your ministry. Be an example to your congregation. Be an example in your speech, in your lifestyle, in everything. If you concentrate on that, God will bless your ministry." Paul did not promise Timothy success numerically, riches, fame, or anything else. He promised that God would use Timothy to accomplish things of everlasting value.

In 1 Corinthians 11:1, the Apostle Paul wrote to the church in Corinth: *Be imitators of me, just as I also am of Christ.* So here we have the model: Christ, who is the ultimate example, and we are all meant to follow his virtues and leadership. Paul wrote to his followers, "Follow me as I follow Christ." So we have Christ; leaders follow him, and their followers go after them. Friends, discipleship happens this way—through the examples we set. Do not underestimate the power of your example. Model the character you want to see in your followers, and the Lord will use it to accomplish his purposes.

Look now at Nehemiah 11:1-24, where Nehemiah and Ezra's courage inspires all of Israel to follow in their steps. In 11:1-2, Nehemiah writes, *And the officials of the people lived in Jerusalem, but the rest of the people cast lots to bring one out of ten to live in Jerusalem, the holy city, while nine-tenths remained in the other cities. And the people blessed all the men who freely offered to live in Jerusalem.* So Nehemiah, Ezra, and the other key leaders set the example. They chose to live in Jerusalem, and, as a result, all the rest of Israel were emboldened. They held a lottery to have one in ten move to Jerusalem. Not everyone was reluctant to go because a lottery was used. No, it was just the opposite.

Everybody wanted to go to Jerusalem to rebuild this nation and be in the capital city. However, they understood that not everybody could go because the surrounding towns and villages needed to be occupied. There were crops to raise and livestock to care for. Only about ten percent of the population could be spared, so they held a lottery. Ten percent of all Israelites would number about four to five thousand people. Verse 2 tells us that those who won the lottery went willingly, and all the remaining Israelites who stayed behind blessed those willing servants. So Nehemiah set the example and encouraged everyone else to follow after. Now Jerusalem would be strengthened and would be a defensible city.

Nehemiah 11:3-24 gives us a listing of the people who made Jerusalem their new home. Verses 10-14 contain a listing of priests, while Verses 15-24 list the Levites and gatekeepers. Notice the caliber of the men who came and joined Nehemiah. Verse 6 calls them *valiant men*, and Verse 14 calls them *mighty men of valor*. These men were bold, courageous, and willing to stare danger in the face to live in Jerusalem despite the threat. They were the kind of men who came to Nehemiah's side. His courage inspired all of them to be courageous.

Now, friends, God might not call you to lead an army into battle or to rebuild a dying nation. But you will be called to lead in some capacity. He may call you to lead a family as a mom or dad, or you might be called to lead a business as an owner or a manager. Maybe you will be called to lead your local church. However God calls you to be a leader, know that he is calling you to lead by example, to set the tempo with your own life and doctrine. For those of you in leadership positions right now, what do you want the people you manage to be like? Parents, think about your children. Managers and business owners, think about those employees under your responsibility. Deacons of the church, think about those church members God has entrusted to your care. What do you want those individuals to be like? What virtues do you want them to embrace? What do you want them to believe? How do you want them to use their lives? Well, become that person yourself. Set an example for them, and then trust that God will use your example to accomplish his purposes. Again, leading by example is the first lesson of godly leadership.

III. Godly leaders have their priorities straight. From the moment he arrived in Jerusalem, Nehemiah's first priority was always Israel's security, which is why his first project was to rebuild Jerusalem's walls. He also stationed guards around Israel, instilled a strict curfew after the walls were built, and locked the doors of Jerusalem every night. Nehemiah made Israel's safety his priority. If he could not guarantee its safety, then nothing else he did would matter. What good would it be to reinstitute temple worship if nobody were safe in worship? What was the point of all the exiles returning to Israel if, the following day, they would be mowed down by their enemies? It all started with security. Everything else came after that. Nehemiah knew the priorities, so he began with safety and security.

The next priority we see is worship. Once Nehemiah had everyone physically secured to the extent that he could, he wanted the Israelites to live for the glory of God, which we see in Nehemiah 11:10-24. Worship had been a vital concern to Nehemiah throughout his time in Israel. However, in 11:10-14, we find that among those people he brought back to Jerusalem were priests who led Israel's worship. In Verses 15 and following, the Levites were recalled to assist the priests. In Verses 19 and following, the temple gatekeepers were recalled to Jerusalem. In Verses 21-22, the overseers of the Levites, temple servants, and singers were recalled to Jerusalem. Now, understand that none of these men were fighters. They were religious leaders. Worship was such a priority to Nehemiah that as these 1 in 10 Israelis were coming into Jerusalem to fortify the city, he wanted to ensure that many of them were also religious leaders. Safety was a major concern for Nehemiah, but so was worship and leading the people to glorify God with their lives.

Friends, as we consider the leadership positions that God has entrusted to us—whether as parents, business leaders, managers, or church leaders—we also need to consider the same priorities. Nehemiah's leadership priorities should always apply to each of us. The first priority is securing the physical safety of those people entrusted to our care. To the greatest extent possible, we must protect the ones God has given us. Our other priorities cannot be accomplished if we cannot protect them. We must keep our people safe. Parents, your responsibility is to protect your kids to the best of your ability. Church leaders, we must make our church building a hardened facility. It must never be a place vulnerable to attack. We must keep our people safe. But then we prioritize worship by leading our people in the Lord's nurture and admonition. We teach them how to live for the glory of God in all of life. My friends, godly leaders set the example and have their priorities straight. At the very top of their priority list are the priorities of safety and worship. Now, we come to a third quality of godly leadership.

IV. Godly leaders care about every person entrusted to them. Every person matters, not just the key players, the young, the healthy, and the strong. Everybody is important. We see this quality in Nehemiah 11:25-36, where Nehemiah listed the towns and villages outside of Jerusalem and the people who lived there. These verses show us that Nehemiah's concern goes beyond just the walls of Jerusalem. Yes, his efforts focused on rebuilding the walls, but his concern was not exclusive to Jerusalem. He was concerned about every last person in Israel because, as governor, he was responsible for them all.

If you look with me at Verse 27, you will notice the town of Beersheba, which is located forty miles south of Jerusalem. Nehemiah knew what was happening in that town as well. As we move into Nehemiah 12, we see a listing of still more people, including the time of their return from exile. So, we read about a listing of priests in 12:1-7, a listing of Levites in Verses 8-9, another listing of high priests in Verses 10-11, and a naming of source books with genealogical records for Israel in Verses 12-21. Friends, as we read through this passage of Scripture, it becomes clear that Nehemiah knew his people, and he knew them well. That intimate knowledge is one of the lessons we can take away from all the lists in the Book of Nehemiah. Have you noticed the long lists of people and places as we have worked through this book? A major takeaway from them is that Nehemiah, the governor of Israel, knew his people. He knew their names, where they lived, their occupations, and the circumstances they were up against.

Friends, we must love and know our people well to be effective and godly leaders. We must show the same concern for them as Nehemiah did for his. Michael Andrew is a man who often writes about leadership. I recently found an article about his father, which he wrote for LinkedIn. His father was a podiatrist, but he remembers the following about his dad: "I assume he was a good doctor technically. I remember the many times I stopped by his office after high school, and, as I waited in the lobby, I invariably heard him engaged in a conversation with a patient. I used to hear conversations about every conceivable topic. They were topics that were important to the patient. What made my father a successful podiatrist was really his ability to relate to each of his patients."

This recollection resonated with me because here we have a doctor who undoubtedly had hundreds and hundreds of patients to look after, and he probably saw dozens of them daily. Yet he took the time to get to know every patient under his care. He learned their names and engaged in small talk with every one of them. He listened to them as they shared with him the important things in their lives—not just the medical needs they came in for, but he wanted to know them as persons. I do not know if this man was a Christian, but his example is what Christian leadership looks like: You know your people, and you love your people. That means you get to know their names and immediate needs, what they do for a living, and what drives them. You know their strengths and weaknesses, their interests, and their hobbies. You learn everything you need to know to be a good leader for them. Friends, this passage is our calling to take a personal interest in every person the Lord gives us to lead.

Parents, let me ask you: How well do you know your children? Do you know their strengths and weaknesses? Do you know what they are going through in school? Do you know all of their hardships? Do you know what drives your kids? Do you know what makes them tick? How well do you know your kids? Do you know what it will take to lead them from where they are now to where they need to be? Business owners and managers, how well do you know your employees? Do you understand what they are going through when they are not on the clock? You need to know the answers to these questions to be a good leader in the workplace. Church leaders, how well do you know the members of your congregation? Do you really know them and their circumstances? Do you know where they live? What is the state of their households? Do you know their struggles? Do you know their victories? Are you able to weep with them as they weep? Are you able to rejoice in their victories? How well do you know your church members? Friends, godly leaders set an example for their people. They know the right priorities and care deeply for every person entrusted to them.

V. Godly leaders celebrate their people's accomplishments. We see this fourth leadership quality in Nehemiah 12:27-43. In this text, Nehemiah hosted a party for Israel to celebrate the completion of Jerusalem's walls, and he clearly spared no expense to make it a party to remember. He had choirs, instrumentalists, singers, and parades. He spared no expense to make it the most lavish celebration Israel had ever seen. He had a parade going in one direction in Jerusalem, another parade going in a different direction, and a third parade going in still another direction. Then, they all met at the Temple in Jerusalem. The party ended with an act of worship as the people offered sacrifices and praise to God. Nehemiah celebrated his people's accomplishments, not in a way that put a spotlight on himself as the leader of all these people. No, the spotlight was on them and what God had done through them. Friends, godly leaders know the importance of celebrating a well-done job. People need to celebrate after a great effort.

If you are a leader and ask your people to give time, money, and energy to a cause, and they buy into the cause and work hard to make the vision a success, then what they need from you in return is an acknowledgment of their service. They need their leader to say, "Yes, I saw that sacrifice. I saw what you did. I saw that you bought into the cause. And I thank God for you." People need and deserve to hear those words of acknowledgment and praise. As godly leaders, we must do that for our people. When we do so, we worship God as the one who gave us such dedicated workers and accomplished something great through them.

Parents, your children need you to celebrate every victory, whether it is the victory of learning how to tie their shoes, graduating from high school, or doing something great. They need to hear you say, "I saw what you did. And I am thrilled for you. I thank God for you." Employers, the employees you are responsible for need you to acknowledge their dedicated service. Maybe they hit their sales target, finished a significant project, or completed the fiscal year under budget. They need to hear you say, "I saw your dedication. I acknowledge it and thank you for it."

When we, as a congregation, set our minds on a significant task and then get it done, there needs to be a celebration for us, too. There needs to be a time when the church leaders, who asked the congregation to sacrifice so much to make it happen, also say thank you for a job well done. Godly leaders celebrate their people. They do not draw attention back to themselves. No, the attention goes solely to those people whom God gave them and who did the work, which leads to our final point.

VI. Godly leaders earn the support of all the people they lead. We see this last quality in Nehemiah 12:44-47, where Nehemiah made a series of leadership appointments. Note these words in Verse 47: *So all Israel in the days of Zerubbabel and Nehemiah were giving the portions due the singers and the gatekeepers as each day required, and set apart the holy portion for the Levites, and the Levites set apart the holy portion for the sons of Aaron.* The idea here is that in the days of Nehemiah, all of Israel fully supported the revitalization efforts. Because Nehemiah had been a great leader, he set the tone with his own example. He got his priorities right and celebrated his people's work. They knew he loved and appreciated them, so they gave their all to the cause. In his day, all of Israel willingly supported the nation, especially its worship.

VII. Conclusion. My friends, now more than ever, we need leaders like Nehemiah. We need his leadership qualities in the Church of Christ—leaders who will lead by example, who have their priorities right, who care about every single person entrusted to their care, who celebrate their people's accomplishments, and who have, therefore, earned the support and trust of everyone they lead. Now, may the Lord grant us such leaders in our day. May he help us to be such leaders in our day.

Chapter Fourteen

REBUILDING OUR VIGILANCE

WE MUST LEARN TO RECOGNIZE THE SIGNS OF SPIRITUAL BACKSLIDING.

I. Introduction to sermon on Nehemiah 13:1-31. This morning marks our last time together in the Book of Nehemiah, so I would like to review where we have been in the series. We learned that Nehemiah was an Israelite living in the heart of Persia about 2,500 years ago and was a very righteous man. When he heard about the terrible state of God's people back in Israel, his heart was broken, so he began to fast, pray, and brainstorm how God might use him to revitalize this nation. Finally, he developed a plan, took it to his boss, King Artaxerxes of Persia, and asked permission to return to his homeland. Artaxerxes listened to the request and granted Nehemiah permission. So Nehemiah made the long 750-mile journey from Susa, where he was based, to Jerusalem in Israel. Artaxerxes appointed Nehemiah governor of the province of Judah, where Jerusalem was located, giving him all the authority he needed to enact his reforms.

After Nehemiah finally arrived in Jerusalem, the first thing he did was assess the state of things. Then, he developed his concrete plan of action. Nehemiah was wise and understood that if Israel were to be revitalized, it had to start with her capital city, which was the heart of her politics, economics, and religious life. He needed to start with Jerusalem. If it were to be revitalized, he would need to begin with her walls. As long as the walls were down, the city was vulnerable to foreign invasion. Nehemiah undertook a massive effort by mobilizing the people of Judah—men, women, and children—to rebuild Jerusalem's walls. It took them many weeks, and they faced all kinds of opposition, but they completed the work and got the walls back up.

Nehemiah's next task was to restore moral integrity to Israel. He learned of a great scandal in Israel during the time the walls were being rebuilt. Some very wealthy Israelites were taking financial advantage of the city's less-fortunate citizens. They extended loans to the poor families of Israel at exorbitant interest rates and accepted their homes and farms as collateral. The rich then seized the homes when these poor citizens could not repay their loans, violating the Law of Moses. It was a tremendous scandal, so Nehemiah needed to tackle it head-on, and he did. He restored the land and the homes of the poor, set up new accountability structures, and ensured that the law of Moses would govern Israel and it would thus be a nation of moral integrity.

After this incident, Nehemiah turned his attention to restoring Israel's corporate worship. He understood that worship fueled reformation and that Israel existed as a nation to worship God and lead other nations to worship. Her worship needed to be restored, and I trust you will remember the first great worship service in Israel. It was organized by Nehemiah and led by Ezra, the scribe. The entire congregation of Israel, about 40,000 people, participated in this grand worship service. Ezra ascended a high wooden platform and took a copy of God's Word with him. As he stood behind his podium and opened God's Word, the congregation of Israel rose to its feet. Ezra then led the congregation in prayer. He prayed to God and thanked him for every instance of his grace to the nation. All the people responded, "Amen, Amen," which meant, "Yes, we affirm everything Ezra said, too."

Then Ezra read from God's Word and expounded it. While he read, many helpers fanned out through this massive crowd. They read what Ezra read and expounded the Scriptures just like Ezra to ensure everybody heard and understood God's Word. As a result of this great worship service, a season of national repentance emerged. All the children of Israel realized how far they had fallen from God's righteous standards. They confessed their sins, showed the fruits of their repentance, went home, enjoyed a grand celebration within their households, and thanked God for his pardon for sin.

After this service, Nehemiah led the people of Israel to renew their national covenant with God. Israel was unique in all of world history because it was founded upon a covenant initiated by God. The Ten Commandments were the foundation of that covenant. However, there were many other statutes and laws, along with promises of blessing for obedience and curses for disobedience. Israel had fallen far from God's standards in that covenant. However, on this occasion, as Israel's worship and moral integrity were restored and she experienced a season of renewed repentance and faith, it was also time to renew the covenant. All of Israel pledged to God that they would be faithful to him. As we closed last week at the end of Nehemiah 12, we saw a grand celebration involving trumpets, choirs, politicians, and priests, with everyone celebrating the restoration of the nation of Israel. Everything was back, and Jerusalem was strong again: Its walls were up, the city was repopulated, its worship was restored, the Temple buzzed with activity, the priesthood was funded, everyone repented and believed in God, and the covenant was renewed. All was well in Israel. It was a grand celebration.

Well, friends, this takes us to today's text in Nehemiah 13, and here is what happened between Chapters 12 and 13. Nehemiah realized his work in Israel was done after the celebration at the end of Chapter 12. King Artaxerxes commissioned him to revitalize Israel, and he realized that he succeeded, which meant it was time for Nehemiah to go home, so that was what he did. Looking at all the fruits of his hard labor, he was pleased that the work had been completed, so he traveled 750 miles back home to be in King Artaxerxes's court again and resumed his job as the king's cupbearer. Nehemiah remained in the heart of Persia for many years, serving faithfully alongside King Artaxerxes. Eventually, however, his heart turned back to his homeland of Israel. I do not know what would have prompted Nehemiah to want to go back. It could have been that he was homesick for Israel or that he was hearing some disturbing reports. Whatever the case might be, after many years at the king's court, he decided to go to Israel again.

Beginning in Nehemiah 13:4, we read about the events after Nehemiah's return. Remember that we do not have a direct sequence of events from Chapter 12 to Chapter 13. Hence, a significant time gap existed during which Nehemiah was in Persia and then returned. As we will see together, the state of Israel left him completely horrified upon Nehemiah's return. He found that Israel was falling back into its old ways once again. Friends, this final chapter of Nehemiah is a cautionary tale about the dangers of spiritual backsliding. It shows us how easy it is to drift away from a commitment to God and fall into sin. It also emphasizes the importance of recognizing the signs of spiritual backsliding so that when they manifest in our lives or church, we can stop them before they go too far. Today's passage highlights four sure signs that we are in spiritual decline. I want to go through each of those four signs this morning, and then we will discuss how to reverse the damage once that backsliding has begun. Here is the first sure sign of backsliding.

II. We are becoming indifferent to worship. Look at Nehemiah 13:4-5 with me: *Now prior to this, Eliashib the priest, who was put in charge over the chambers of the house of our God, being related to Tobiah, had prepared a large room for him, where formerly they put the grain offerings, the frankincense, the utensils, and the tithes of grain, also new wine and oil commanded for the Levites, the singers, and the gatekeepers, as well as the contributions for the priests.* Nehemiah had been gone a long time—years and years. He returned to Israel, and his first stop was the Temple of Jerusalem, which showed his spiritual zeal. The first thing he wanted to see upon his return to Israel was the house of God, but when he got there, what did he find? An abomination: Tobiah the Ammonite, the same Tobiah we encountered in Chapter 2, had turned the Temple of God into his own private residence, the same Tobiah who was so angry at Nehemiah for rebuilding Jerusalem's walls that he organized a group of soldiers to harass, demean, and threaten the workers. He even hatched a plot to murder Nehemiah. So, Nehemiah returned and found Tobiah living in the Temple. How could this happen?

According to Verse 4, Tobiah was related to Eliashib, the priest, probably through marriage. One of Tobiah's children or grandchildren had married one of Eliashib's children or grandchildren, so the priest was related to this pagan governor. Somehow, during Nehemiah's absence, Tobiah convinced his relation to clear out one of the temple chambers so he could live there, and this conviction most likely occurred slowly over time. Perhaps after Nehemiah left, Tobiah renewed his acquaintance with Eliashib. It may have started with exchanging letters, or maybe Tobiah started visiting Jerusalem to see some of his family. From there, it might have turned into overnight stays, which became more frequent. Finally, Tobiah might have sealed the deal by discussing the situation with Eliashib in a conversation that may have happened as follows:

TOBIAH: "I do not want to keep putting you people out when I make my visits. Would it not be nice for me to have an apartment or something here in Jerusalem where I could stay during my visits?"

ELIASHIB: "That does sound like a good idea, Tobiah, but where should we put you up?"

TOBIAH: "We have an unused old storage room at the Temple. Why not clear it out? I can throw a cot in there, and that will work fine."

ELIASHIB: "That sounds like a good idea to me."

Before long, the Israelites had the governor of a pagan people living in the holiest site in Israel. Indeed, it was the most sacred site on all of planet Earth—where God physically manifested his presence.

Now, friends, there is a reason why we call "spiritual backsliding" the condition in which one's faith and devotion to God grows cold. It does not happen in one great leap. You do not go from being a committed believer to a committed apostate in one fell swoop. It happens very slowly over time. One small compromise leads to another small compromise. One little concession to the world of unbelief leads to another concession, and then another, until you end up where you never imagined you would be. That is how backsliding occurs: one little compromise at a time. Friends, spiritual backsliding can happen to individuals, local churches, and entire denominations. The solution is this: Those believers with some remaining spiritual zeal need the courage to confront the backsliders and call their brothers and sisters back to faithfulness.

Nehemiah recorded his response to this situation in 13:8-9, where he wrote, *It was very evil to me*. His response was precisely the correct one: righteous anger at seeing the holiest site of Israel turned into the dwelling place of a pagan leader. He should have been angry, as he wrote in Verse 9, that, in his anger, he threw all Tobiah's household furniture out of the chamber: *Then I said the word, and they cleansed the chambers; and I returned there the utensils of the house of God with the grain offerings and the frankincense*. He was so filled with godly zeal that he could not help but reverse the damage done, so he plowed into Tobiah's chamber, threw the furniture out, restored all the items for worship, and insisted that the Temple should be used to worship God from then on.

This scene reminds me of the great event in Christ's earthly ministry when he visited the Temple in Jerusalem. Do you remember that story? He entered the Temple and saw that instead of worship, there were all these money changers buying, selling, and making a significant profit. They slapped each other on the back while farm animals milled about the temple courtyards. Our Lord was so furious that he twisted a whip and began beating those who were misusing the Lord's Temple. He overturned the tables and said in Matthew 21:13, *"It is written, 'My house shall be called a house of prayer'; but you are making it a robbers' den."* Nehemiah's action foreshadowed our Lord's great cleansing of the Temple.

Friends, when we are backsliding, we need someone like Nehemiah to confront us, shake us out of our complacency, and rekindle our desire for faithfulness to God's Word. Here is the first sign of spiritual backsliding: We become indifferent to God's worship. A place once dedicated to worship is turned into the dwelling place of a pagan. God forbid that our church, a place dedicated to God's worship, should ever be detracted from its purpose because of her people's spiritual indifference. Now, we turn to the second sign of spiritual backsliding.

III. We are no longer giving to the Lord's cause (or at least not like we used to). Spiritual backsliding occurs when we no longer concern ourselves with pure worship and no longer give to the Lord's cause like we used to. Look at Nehemiah 13:10 with me: *I also came to know.* Let me stop there; is that not a tragic statement? Nehemiah invested so much of his life into the reformation of Israel. At the time he departed, it was perfect. However, he came back years later, and it was bad enough that Tobiah was living in the Temple. However, he also found other problems, including a series of outrages in Israel.

In Verse 10, he discovered something else: *I also came to know that the portions of the Levites had not been given them, so the Levites and the singers who did the work had fled, each to his own field.* Before Nehemiah left, the Israelites promised to support these religious workers. According to Chapter 12, they generously supplied the Levites and the singers, who were dedicated to temple worship, with everything they needed so their full-time occupation could be serving in the Temple. But, during Nehemiah's absence, the Israelites decided that supporting the Levites and singers was too significant a burden for them. I am sure they had all kinds of excuses. Perhaps they said, "Well, Nehemiah, the economy was roaring back then. Now, the economy is in shambles. We cannot give anymore." Or maybe they said, "Nehemiah, we have had a few bad years with our crops. There is no surplus to give." They gave all kinds of good excuses, but that was all they were. The truth was that the Israelites did not want to part with their resources, so the Levites began fending for themselves, which meant they were forced to leave the temple precincts. They needed to find homes, raise crops, and support themselves.

Of course, these consequences meant that temple worship was no longer taking place—no wonder Tobiah could get a room in the temple chamber. The priests no longer needed a room to store all their offerings for worship, because nobody made any offerings for worship. And the Levites were not being supported, so they were forced to help themselves. As a result, the Lord's work could not be fully carried out in Israel anymore. In 13:11-13, Nehemiah, once again, confronted the offenders by compelling them to start giving again. He then set up new accountability structures to handle the donations properly. One sure sign that we are spiritually backsliding is when we become indifferent to worship. Another sure sign is that we direct fewer of our resources to the Lord's work, and our excuses for not doing so may sound like this: "Well, I would if I had more. If the Lord blessed me, I would happily give back to him." When our excuses mount and our generosity decreases, we know we are in a state of backsliding. Now, let us examine a third sign of spiritual backsliding in this text.

IV. We are misusing the Lord's Day. Look at Nehemiah 13:15-16 with me: *In those days I saw in Judah some who were treading wine presses on the sabbath, and bringing in sacks of grain and loading them on donkeys, as well as wine, grapes, figs and all kinds of loads, and they brought them into Jerusalem on the sabbath day. So, I testified against them on the day they sold food. Also men of Tyre were living there who brought in fish and all kinds of merchandise, and sold them to the sons of Judah on the sabbath, even in Jerusalem.* Now, friends, earlier, the Israelites promised to keep the Sabbath day holy, just as the law of Moses prescribed. They would not buy, sell, or manufacture; they would use the Sabbath day for rest and worship. That was their pledge. But look at the Israelites now: Wine, grapes, figs, fish, textiles, and more were being bought, sold, and manufactured on the Sabbath day.

Once again, I would have bet the Israelites made all kinds of good excuses. They probably said to Nehemiah, "Yes, Nehemiah. We are Jews. We observe the Sabbath. But you know, all the nations around us are not Jewish. They work on the Sabbath. Suppose we do not open for business on the Sabbath. In that case, the nations around us will take their business elsewhere, so we either do this on the Sabbath, or we cannot do it at all." I am sure they brought up the state of the economy to Nehemiah and said, "Times are really tough. Six days of work are not enough to cover the bills anymore. We need to work all seven days." They created all kinds of excuses, but in Verse 17, Nehemiah calls it evil. In Verse 18, he says they are *profaning the sabbath*, which means they are taking something holy and treating it as if it were vulgar.

Nehemiah then confronted them again in Verse 19, where he wrote, *Now it happened that just as it grew dark at the gates of Jerusalem before the sabbath, I said the word, and the doors were shut. Then I said that they should not open them until after the sabbath. Then I had some of my young men stand at the gates so that no load would enter on the sabbath day.* So Nehemiah confronted the Israelites for profaning the Sabbath, ignored their excuses, and said, "No, this is a moral issue. You are doing evil in the sight of God." Then, as the governor of Judah, he ordered that the gates of Jerusalem should be locked before the Sabbath began and remained locked until the Sabbath was over. That way, nobody could come in, and nobody could go out. There would be no more buying and selling on the Sabbath day.

Now, friends, we might not be under the Law of Moses today, but we are under the Law of Christ, which declares that God's people must gather on the first day of every week. We must pray, sing, and read God's Word together when we gather. We must hear God's Word expounded, regularly baptize our new converts, and participate in the Lord's Supper. It is a sure sign that we are spiritually backsliding if Sunday morning ceases to be the most important time on our calendars.

Over the years, I have heard many excuses from able-bodied people as to why they cannot make it to Sunday morning worship. One man told me, "My son has baseball practice on Sunday mornings, and we cannot very well miss baseball practice." God forbid we miss the opportunity to bat around a ball on a field when we can worship God and fellowship with his people instead. We do not want to miss our game for something like worship. Here is the most common excuse I have heard: "Pastor, we are swamped right now. We work our tails off Monday through Saturday, so we need to sleep in on Sunday. It would be too difficult to wake up early Sunday, go to church, and then take an afternoon nap." Their decision was made: They would skip the worship altogether.

My friends, these excuses are for the backslidden. We need someone like Nehemiah to confront us head-on and say "No" when they come. This issue is a moral one. God tells his people to gather on the first day of the week because he deserves our worship, and we need each other for fellowship and accountability. We need someone like Nehemiah to shake us out of spiritual lethargy. Now, let us address the fourth sure sign of spiritual backsliding, which incorporates all the others.

V. We are falling in love with the world. Look at Nehemiah 13:23-24 with me: *In those days I also saw that the Jews had married women from Ashdod, Ammon, and Moab. As for their children, half spoke in the language of Ashdod, and none of them was able to speak the language of Judah, but only the tongue of his own people.* Well, friends, this might have been the Israelites' most tragic scenario. When Nehemiah departed from Israel many years ago, the people put away all forms of paganism. They vowed before God that they would not give their sons and daughters in marriage to a pagan people because they understood that a pagan rarely converts to the true religion of God. More often, the true believer is brought over to the pagan side of the world.

They vowed they would not let this happen, but their attitude changed at some point during these long years of Nehemiah's absence. Once again, the sons and daughters of Israel were given in marriage to the sons and daughters of the pagan nations around them, and the result was predictable: The pagans were not won over to Judaism. The Jews were won over to paganism. Children were born to these couples, and the children grew up learning to speak the language of the pagan nations around them but not knowing how to speak the Hebrew language of Israel. And friends, understand what the significance of this would be. If a generation of children grew up not even knowing the Hebrew language, it meant they would never hear the Word of God as it was read, nor could they read it for themselves. They could no longer sing the worship songs of Israel, listen to a sermon, or learn the ways of God. The religious extinction of God's people was at stake.

I found this quote from Derek Kidner compelling: "A single generation's compromise could undo the work of centuries." My pastor, Steve Thomas, said, "The church is always just one generation away from extinction." Is that not true? The faith can be perpetuated from one generation to the next for millennia. However, all it takes is just one generation to say, "This is not worth our time," and then to decide they will not raise their kids in the nurture and admonition of the Lord. It takes only one generation to say, "We are not going to worship anymore or give to the cause of God. We are not making this a priority and will not read the Scriptures together anymore." It takes only one generation to adopt these habits, and the church becomes extinct.

This concern explains Nehemiah's dramatic response in Verse 25, where he wrote, *So I contended with them and cursed them.* That meant he pronounced God's judgment on them, and he *struck some of them and pulled out their hair.* Nehemiah designed these responses to shame the guilty parties publicly. He continued in Verse 25: *And [I] struck some of them and pulled out their hair and made them swear by God, "You shall not give your daughters to their sons, nor take up their daughters for your sons or for yourselves."* Now, friends, Nehemiah's response may seem harsh, and indeed it was, but I believe he would say to us that desperate times call for desperate measures. The people of God were on the verge of going extinct. One generation raised like this would not know the Word of God and have no ability to read it. The faith would stop, and Israel would cease to exist as a light to the nations of the world. It would all be over. The Law of Moses threatened the destruction of Israel if they continued in practices like this. So Nehemiah, as the governor of Judah, decided that the only way to get through to his lawless citizens was through corporal punishment and public shaming, and that was what he did. It might shake them out of their complacency.

In Nehemiah 13:28, we find an equally shocking scenario: *And even one of the sons of Joiada, the son of Eliashib the high priest, was a son-in-law of Sanballat the Horonite, so I made him flee away from me.* Do you remember Sanballat the Horonite? He was one of these other guys who, along with Tobiah, tried to kill Nehemiah and stop the revitalization of Israel. Now, he was related to the high priest of Israel through intermarriage, so the nation was being corrupted, and the priesthood would be lost. Nehemiah's reaction was recorded in Verse 29: *Remember them, O my God, because they have defiled the priesthood and the covenant of the priesthood and the Levites.* So Nehemiah cleansed it all. In Verses 30-31, he spoke not in racial but religious terms. Everything smacked of paganism, so he cleansed it from Israel. And then, the book ends with a prayer, where Nehemiah prayed, "God, remember that I tried my best. I tried my best to reform your people."

VI. Conclusion and final applications. Friends, 1 John 2:17 states the following: *The will of God abides forever.* We must be aware of the dangers involved with spiritual backsliding and the spiritual drift that can lead us away from our love of God and into our love of the world. We must beware of that pull away from God that we feel every time we are tempted not to participate in public worship and when we are tempted to hoard our resources instead of giving them to his work, when we feel the temptation to violate the laws of God, when we are tempted to join hands with the world rather than to be a prophetic voice within the world, and when we misuse the Lord's day. We must resist the temptation to backslide spiritually. Suppose we give in to this temptation and drift away from the Lord. In that case, we are condemning ourselves and our posterity after us to life without God and all the blessings that come from it. Of course, as we have seen, the solution is for people like Nehemiah, with some spiritual zeal and moral courage remaining, to confront backsliding when they see it. We need courageous people to confront their children and fellow church members. We need church leaders who will confront their church members when they see signs of spiritual apathy and a drifting away from the things of God. We need Nehemiahs who will call God's people back to faithfulness and do everything they can to bring them back.

There is another way to prevent spiritual backsliding, and that is through spiritual watchfulness. Every one of us needs to learn it. Friends, we need some Nehemiahs among us—people with the courage to confront the backsliders with gentleness and respect but to engage them nonetheless. But then, we must all learn to be watchful of our own souls. For starters, we can do so through prayer by constantly going to God and asking him to keep our conscience sensitive and to keep our desire for him strong so that we will not drift. We must be in the Scriptures often so that God's Word can do its work within us. And friends, we must guard our hearts, which means guarding the gateways into our hearts by filtering what we set before our eyes. We need to be like King David, who wrote in Psalm 101:3, *I will set no vile thing before my eyes*. That verse would be a good one to place on our television sets and computer screens. Maybe we should put it on our phone cases to remind ourselves that we must not look at that which is evil and be careful what we hear through our ears, as well as what we do with our hands and feet, where we go, and how we occupy ourselves. We must always be mindful of what we do, see, hear, and expose ourselves to.

Now, there are some things in this world that we cannot guard ourselves against. When you go to work, your co-workers will do what they will do. You cannot prevent their actions, but you can control what you entertain yourself with at home. You can also control who your closest friends will be, what you will put before your eyes, what you will listen to with your ears, and what literature you will read. My friend, you must be spiritually watchful and make sure that while you are educated about the world, you do not cause yourself to get interested in what the world offers and that its vain philosophies do not tempt you. Finally, we must keep close to our local church and stay connected to people like Nehemiah, who will hold us accountable for our actions. Friends, the Book of Nehemiah ends with a cautionary tale to help us avoid making the same mistake the ancient Israelites made.

ABOUT THE AUTHOR

Dr. Brandon J. Crawford has been the Lead Pastor of a Bible-believing, Christ-centered church in Marshall, Michigan, since 2010. He holds the Master of Divinity degree from Detroit Baptist Theological Seminary (Allen Park, Michigan) and the Master of Theology and Doctor of Philosophy degrees from Puritan Reformed Theological Seminary (Grand Rapids, Michigan).

As lead pastor, Dr. Crawford oversees the discipleship of the church's congregation and its outreach into the community. He engages in weekly preaching and teaching, administers the ordinances of baptism and communion, provides spiritual counsel to individuals and families, supervises the various ministries of our church, and ensures that the church remains faithful to its identity, mission, vision, and values.

In addition to his pastoral responsibilities, Dr. Crawford also regularly contributes to the city's local newspaper, to magazines, books, and academic journals, and he serves as a community chaplain. He and his wife were married in 2006, and they have two children.